Sweet Adeline

A Journey through Care

Patricia Slack

and

Frank Mulville

**MACMILLAN
EDUCATION**

First published 1988

Published by
MACMILLAN EDUCATION LTD
Houndmills, Basingstoke, Hampshire RG21 2XS
and London
Companies and representatives
throughout the world

Typeset by Wessex Typesetters
(Division of The Eastern Press Ltd)
Frome, Somerset

Printed in Hong Kong

ISBN 0–333–46251–3

1590548

Other books published by Patricia Slack and Frank Mulville

Patricia Slack, *School Nursing*, Baillière Tindall (1978)

Frank Mulville, *Terschelling Sands*, Herbert Jenkins (1968) and Conway Maritime Press (1987)

Frank Mulville, *In Granma's Wake*, Seafarer Books (1970)

Frank Mulville, *Rustler on the Beach*, Angus and Robertson (1976)

Frank Mulville, *Schooner Integrity*, Seafarer Books (1979)

Frank Mulville, *Single-handed Cruising and Sailing*, Macmillan (1981)

To everyone who loved Adeline and helped us to care for her

'The clouds you so much dread
are big with mercy, and shall break
In blessings on your head'
William Cowper

Contents

Preface

This story of the last six years of my mother's life began when she was still active and reasonably healthy. She suffered a severe stroke and was not expected to survive—but she did. She rallied to find herself severely disabled, in a wheelchair, unable to read, write or speak except to say "do, da, do" in response to everything.

The event devastated my mother, myself and Frank. We lived through the emotional trauma of her disablement, of poor hospital care and of having to decide on her future long-term care. At first we maintained her in her own home, in the north of England, two hundred miles from London where we lived and worked. Eventually, through many vicissitudes, all three of us survived to live happily in the same house.

We learnt how to manage as we went along. Useful information was difficult to find. I seized on the experiences of other carers for the practical details outside the experience of professionals and missing from the books they write. I found that carers' accounts of the emotions surrounding their experiences helped me to grapple with the cauldron of love, remorse, anger, fear, hatred and violence which boiled inside me. I sat late into the night reading Dervla Murphy's autobiography *Wheels within Wheels*, part of which describes her caring experiences in heart-rending detail, and found it more comforting and refreshing than sleep.

I too wanted to share our experiences but I did not want to hurt or embarrass my mother. I explained to her what I wanted to do and I believe that she supported the idea of this book, feeling that her tortuous experience would have been justified if it could be of use to others. In some strange, inexplicable way I feel she helped to write it.

Severe handicap can tear families apart and destroy relationships. Because the attitudes and response of every member of the family affects a dependant's care, Frank and I have written this book together from our different points of view. We have tried to combine practical details with the story of our experience and the emotions it produced. I hope it will help other carers and give professionals a glimpse into the problems and feelings of the patients and relatives they meet.

Learning through experience takes time and therefore some of the practical information is spread over several chapters. To help consolidate and include extra points we have added a chapter 'Points for Carers' at the end. It concentrates on the details sparsely covered or missing from other books.

We have left some of the characters nameless or given them fictitious names as we have no wish to hurt any of those involved in the story. We do not believe anyone intended to hurt us but they often did and we have presented events as they seemed to us at the time. The story has been reconstructed from journals and diaries kept throughout the period and from notes my mother's helpers and I wrote to keep us informed. In re-reading these journals we were surprised how much our perceptions of events had altered and how we had forgotten most of 1982—our worst year.

Caring for a severely disabled relative is demanding and exhausting, as so often depicted by the media. We hear little about the rewards. My mother showed Frank and me a new depth and breadth of love for each other. Her tragedy formed the basis for the most enriching emotional experience of our lives. Caring is a challenge, with rewards for those who take heart and shoulder it successfully. We hope this book will help.

August, 1987   P.S.
                                                                 F.M.

Acknowledgements

The authors and publishers wish to thank *Nursing Times* for permission to reproduce the cover photograph and photographs on pages 84, 97 and 152, as well as the letter on page 183.

1 Prelude

Wendy writes up to December 1980

I used to think it began with my mother's stroke. Now I believe it began when I was four and she took a job as a housekeeper looking after old blind Mrs Toller. At first, Mrs Toller called me 'the awful child' but we were soon firm friends and I spent hours curled up on the settee beside her. She had once been a well-known flower illustrator and, despite her blindness, she taught me to draw snowdrops. I can see us now—heads bent over the paper as her deft fingers guided the pencil unseeingly to the right place.

My grandmother was the next old lady in my life. I was six when she fell and broke her hip and then developed pneumonia. My mother and I left Mrs Toller and went back to the farmhouse in Ireland to look after her. It was twelve years before she died. I remember her as rather a cross old granny but she and I played draughts, snakes and ladders, and snap. I retrieved the dropped stitches in her knitting and we both laughed when we searched for her glasses only to find them sitting on her forehead.

For warmth and comfort and cuddles I used to run across the fields to the next farm where old blind Maggie sat fanning the fire in the open hearth. Blind Maggie always greeted me with surprise and joy and felt me all over before pronouncing me to be Wendy. I sat on a stool by the fire while Maggie brushed and plaited my long red hair. Maggie's niece fed us with mugs of tea and hot bread straight out of the pan which hung over the open fire.

As Granny grew older, she became more helpless. She was often incontinent and she needed help to wash and dress. I helped by finding clothes, tying laces, brushing hair and fetching water to and from her room as my mother was busy housekeeping and helping with the farm. It was all part of our daily life. In our countryside, people led healthy lives and lived to an old age. There were plenty of old people and they all lived at home until they died. Even in 1945 there must have been alternatives but I never heard them discussed. The state did not supply wheelchairs, handicap aids or attendance allowance. No one paid an insurance stamp for my mother. The farm belonged to my uncle. My father reneged on his maintenance; so my mother had little money, no help and no recreation. It was a tough life for her but I was happy. I wonder now what she could have got out of it. Granny was difficult and unappreciative. For all that, in later life my mother recalled those years nostalgically.

Nevertheless, she warned, "Don't ever do this for me. If I become helpless and handicapped, put me in a home and forget about me. Don't ruin your life."

I paid no heed—my mother would never grow old

2

I paid no heed—my mother would never grow old. I lived suspended in a life of sunny days and harvesting, of joyous cycle rides through the crisp sharp autumn air to school, of donkey races with school friends and sandwiches in winter round the classroom fire.

I was eleven when I won a scholarship to boarding school. Inevitably I saw less of Granny, and old Maggie had died. I helped vaguely in school holidays, resenting Granny as she gradually declined into a world of senility, incontinence and helplessness. I fed her and helped to change the sheets. I wished she would die and set my mother free. When I finally stood by her open grave on that bitterly cold January afternoon I felt no regret or sorrow. It was to be thirty years before I recalled the games and happiness we shared in my early childhood years.

I was thirty-nine when I met Frank. He came at the end of a long line of broken relationships. He was fun, dependable, adventurous and he made me happy. He was also married. I had a good life with plenty of friends, enough money, a good job and a tiny flat in London. I was also emotionally insecure and lonely.

I often visited my mother, now widowed and a retired ward sister living in the north of England. Sometimes she came on the bus to see me. She was still poor but proud with strict moral standards. She had disapproved of every man in my life and I had come to expect an introduction to my mother as the beginning of the end of a promising relationship. For all that, I loved my mother and enjoyed seeing her. This time I resolved to keep Frank a secret.

Frank spent most of his free time sailing. He had a reputation for single-handed ocean sailing and he earned part of his living writing about it. I was soon spending most of my weekends on his boat *Iskra*. I hardly noticed how little I saw of my mother. When I did, she wanted to discuss her funeral arrangements, where her small savings were invested and what I should do with her belongings when she died. I dismissed this as morbid, saying she looked and acted far younger than her age—which she did. My thoughts were too occupied with Frank to pay attention.

Frank's book *Schooner Integrity* was published in the autumn of 1979. As part of the publisher's launch, he brought *Iskra* to St Katherine's dock in London. During this time, my mother arrived for a weekend and, nagged by Frank, I invited him to dinner to meet her. They got on well and the following day he invited us to have coffee on board the boat. On the way home my mother remarked on the orderliness of the boat—it was clear that as a meticulous, tidy person she was impressed. The extent of my relationship with Frank was not mentioned.

The following year, disillusioned with his book's sales in the USA, Frank packed 800 of his books into *Iskra* and sailed to America. I joined him for a holiday in the Azores and again for a three-week cruise along the New England coast. It was before that last holiday that I received a bitter letter from my mother urging me to drop the relationship. I ignored it and flew to America but I felt guilty and eventually showed the letter to Frank. He was furious. It was the only nasty letter I ever received from my mother in the hundreds she wrote to me but it was to colour Frank's view of her for years.

I spent August Bank Holiday with my mother. I was surprised to see her pale and tired and shocked when the doctor telephoned to say she must go into hospital on Bank Holiday Monday to have severe anaemia investigated. She finally admitted she had stopped taking her iron tablets a year ago because they made her sick and she was tired of taking tablets. This seemed an odd thing for a nurse to do and I wonder now whether it was an expression of a growing sense of loneliness and loss of anything to live for. It was not the sort of thing she would have discussed with me but, if I had pangs of guilt because I had neglected her, I have forgotten them now.

There were few preparations to be made as my mother was always prepared for any emergency. She kept a case packed with clean nighties, a towel, washing things, a small jar of sugar, a table napkin, writing paper, pre-stamped envelopes and a list of jobs to be done before leaving the house—turn off the electricity, shut all windows, lock the back door, and so on.

She seemed nervous when I took her to the hospital on Monday afternoon. I waited until she was undressed and settled in bed.

I tried to reassure her. "It's nothing at all. You've always been anaemic; as soon as you start taking your tablets again, you'll be as right as rain."

I arranged some roses from the garden and left them on her locker, promising to come back from London next weekend.

At first it was not too bad. She came home at weekends and I travelled north to be with her. There were minor irritations—the

4

ward was grubby, the bath badly stained, and the dinners always accompanied by chips and gravy which she hated. There was no ward telephone; so she had to go down a flight of stairs to a call-box in a draughty corridor and fix a time to telephone me. There was a student nurses' prank in which she was sprayed with water while sitting on the lavatory, but there was always the weekend to look forward to.

She told me she had had several tests and had seen two consultants, neither of whom seemed able to diagnose the problem. She had a course of iron injections followed by iron tablets but they seemed to have little effect. She was critical of the poor nursing care she observed. My mother had been a strict, dedicated ward sister and it horrified her to see ill patients unfed and incontinent patients left lying in wet beds. There was no shortage of staff—it was sloppy and badly supervised practice. She tried to help some of the ill patients and may have made herself unpopular with the staff.

Then she was too ill to come home. She had been vomiting all day one Friday and I found her in bed, pale and eyes closed against the light. Her left eye looked swollen and she said it throbbed painfully. Staff nurse said the doctor had seen what she had vomited but had not examined her—seeing her eyes closed, he had thought she was asleep.

On Saturday, she was worse. Now the pain had spread all over the left side of her face to her ear, sinus and teeth, and she said she felt as though she had an abscess behind her eye. She was having strong pain killers and drank only a little milk and glucose.

Despite her illness, nothing seemed to be happening.

"When is the doctor coming?" I enquired of sister.

"Oh, there won't be anyone here now until Monday," she said. "It's rather awkward really as the consultant is on holiday, the new senior doctor has not yet arrived and the house doctor is off duty."

"But surely", I said, "she's not going to be left like this all weekend?"

"Oh stop worrying," she said. "We'll get it sorted out on Monday."

I spent a restless night. What was wrong with her? An abscess? Acute glaucoma? Suppose it was meningitis? I went downstairs to consult my old nursing books. I went back to bed and fell into a fitful doze punctuated by sickening dreams—she was dying; she was dead. I was complaining to the consultant. I was insulting the ward sister. The ward sister had been dismissed. I woke up, made some tea and took it back to bed. I mulled over the various stories my mother had told me about the ward, for the first time taking them seriously. It was ridiculous not to be able to get a doctor in a hospital. Had she been at home, I would have called the family doctor.

I was back in the ward by 9 am. My mother was still in pain and I asked the staff nurse in charge if she would call a doctor—any doctor. My mother's eye was pouring fluid and I asked whether it could be bathed and have an eye pad to mop up the moisture and to keep out the light which hurt badly. This turned out to be difficult. It seemed that, because this was not an eye ward, there were no suitable prepared sterile trays for eye bathing and no eye shades or pads. They managed a compromise by finding a piece of lint to cover the eye.

"What do you want me to do?" asked the doctor when he arrived.

"Find out what is wrong with my mother and give her some treatment," I replied.

"You realise the laboratories are closed for the weekend? There's nothing I can do," he said.

"But surely you could examine her?" I persisted.

"No need," he said. " 'Suspected rheumatic sinusitis' is written in the notes but I will speak to the house doctor tomorrow."

I felt angry, upset and helpless. His casual air of superiority told me he regarded me as an interfering relative to be snubbed and subordinated. I felt that, far from helping my mother, I had increased antipathy against her. With an aching heart, I said goodbye to her to catch the train to London.

Without a patients' telephone, we were cut off from each other. It would be five days before I could get back to the area and speak to her again. On Monday, when I rang, sister told me the doctor had diagnosed shingles which was being treated but my mother was still ill. Each time I rang I asked the staff to tell her but it seemed few of these messages got through. I wanted to talk to her, to hear her voice and to comfort her. A patients' telephone would have helped us both.

On Tuesday evening a friend Jill Riley telephoned to tell me she was worried as my mother seemed to be having nothing to eat.

Lunch was stew and chips which she was too sick to consider and nothing was offered instead. I could stand it no longer. I rang my editor. Alison listened.

"You must go back," she said. "Don't worry. Do what you have to do and we'll sort out the time later."

On Wednesday I was due to report a top National Health Service (NHS) management conference about reorganisation of the health service. I called in at the conference hall on my way to the train to ask a colleague to take over for me. I stood waiting at the entrance and watching these well-dressed confident managers chatting and laughing over cups of coffee. I hated them—I knew this expensive conference charade would change nothing for my mother.

I found her huddled in bed, pale and still. Both eyes were shut—one with shingles, and the other infected. Black scabs covered the left side of her nose, her eye and forehead up into her hair. She turned unseeingly towards me and squeezed my hand. As I sat by her bed in the afternoon, she dozed fitfully. Bit by bit a sorry tale emerged.

It seemed the consultant had been to see her and told her she was still not responding to the iron and would have to have a blood transfusion. Hardly surprising, I thought, considering she had been sickening for shingles and vomiting for a week with little to eat or drink. He arranged for the eye consultant to visit her as she was too ill to travel to the eye clinic at another hospital. However, the eye consultant found he could not come and so my mother was sent by ambulance to the clinic at the other side of town. She was sick and vomited throughout the journey which was protracted as the ambulance stopped to collect other patients. When they finally arrived at the clinic, no wheelchair could be found. She would have to walk. Her legs kept collapsing and two of the nurses half carried and half dragged her to the waiting room. There was a two-hour wait during which the sickness subsided but she was exhausted and thirsty. She would have liked to lie down and wanted a drink but there was no bed or trolley and no refreshments. She finally saw the doctor who prescribed ointment and drops and said it would take three weeks for the eye to heal. She arrived back in her bed after the last meal was served at 5.30 pm and fell into an exhausted sleep. Another day had passed without food or drink.

I was furious but she held on to my hand.

"Promise you won't complain. Please, please don't," she pleaded. "They'll take it out on me and make it worse. We'll get through somehow but please, please don't say anything."

I ached all over with rage, fury and hatred for these people. Most of all I hated this thin, rat-faced demi-god of a ward sister who somehow got away with running an outfit more suited to a torture chamber than a hospital.

I went back to my mother's house and made a baked custard which I took into the hospital. She ate half of it along with some jelly one of the nurses brought her. Whatever else may have been wrong with the ward, they allowed me to visit at any time for as long as I liked. When I visited the ward next morning, she looked a little better and had had some porridge for breakfast.

I saw the consultant who repeated that she was not responding to the iron but, although he suspected cancer, all the tests were clear. He planned to repeat some of them when she recovered from shingles. I asked whether he could order her a light diet as she could not eat the stew, chips and bully beef with a sick stomach.

"There is no special diet," he said. "She can have anything she likes. She only has to ask."

"So far, it seems difficult to have anything other than the set meal," I persisted.

"Nonsense," he replied. "There's plenty of food—anything she fancies."

He was either hopelessly out of touch with what happened on his ward or he preferred not to know.

He fobbed off any suggestion that the nursing care was poor. "It's not like when your mother was a ward sister, you know. Things have changed and you have to accept that."

I was not willing to accept it but at the same time I did not want to alienate him. He was the only member of staff I had any rapport with and he was the most powerful. I did not want to argue with him.

At 11.30 am the hospital served lunch—the main meal of the day. I had brought another baked custard and I went back into the ward and fed it to my mother—she could not see to feed herself properly. As I left the hospital, I bumped into the consultant again and we walked together to the gate.

"What is her prognosis?" I asked, the tears starting to roll down my face.

He put his hand on my shoulder—a gesture of warmth too much for me in a sea of indifference and pain. "I don't know—she is very ill," he replied.

"If she's going to die, I'd rather she died at home," I wept.

"Look, my dear," he said, "I have plenty of hope but, if it comes to that, I'll see she comes home."

Still weeping, I walked back to my mother's house through the streets in the bright October sunshine. It was the sort of sunny autumn day my mother loved. Had she been at home, we would have had lunch under the plum tree. I dropped into the newspaper shop. Mr Lewis noticed my tear-stained face but passed no remark.

Instead he called out cheerily, "I've found a chap to clear the garden for you. She'll want it nice when she comes home."

Her garden was her pride and joy.

She was asleep when I got back to the ward in the afternoon. I sat by her bed and read the newspaper until she woke. She seemed dazed and drugged but listened while I told her about the garden and the house. She took some of the fresh orange juice and barley drink I had made her and asked me to stay and feed her at supper time. She ate another baked custard with some ice cream and I sat with her until the nurses came to wash her. As I got up to leave, she started to weep. Only once as a child had I seen her cry.

Between hospital visits there was plenty to do. I had brought several pieces of work from my office and I was writing an article about the Boynton committee report on the poor standards of care at Rampton Hospital, with a deadline to meet. I sat up late and rose early to finish the article, to deal with my office work and to write letters to friends and relatives.

Frank was still in America. He had written and telephoned to say he was coming home and I wrote him a long, tearful letter. I felt very alone and helpless. I wanted someone to tell me what to do. I had no friends of my own in the north and so I rang Jill Riley. Jill, although my own age, was an old friend of my mother. They had become friends when my mother retired from her job and advertised herself as a baby-sitter. Jill was among those who replied and for years my mother went every Saturday night to look after the children Malcolm and Alison, while Jill and Steve went out. When I was staying with my mother, I went too. We had spent many happy evenings with the children and watched them grow up. Alison, now eleven, was a loyal friend of my mother, and she and Jill visited her in hospital almost every day.

I talked to Jill for a long time. What did she think I ought to do? I needed to get back to my job in London but I was frightened to leave my mother. At least, if I was in the area, I knew what was going on, and I could cook food which she could eat. I could bring her nourishing drinks and feed her while she could not see. The doctor had said it would take three weeks to heal. One week had already gone—she must be able to open her eyes soon. Jill thought I ought to visit until she was eating better and could see to feed herself.

She did indeed improve. During the next two days, I brought her minced chicken, steamed fish and more baked custards which she seemed to like. Her right eye opened and she could see to feed herself. She started to eat some of the hospital food and she was sitting out of bed in a chair. She could not manage to read and the only programme on the hospital radio was pop music. She enjoyed listening to Radio 3 and 4; so I brought in her small radio with an ear-piece—it would not disturb other patients but take her mind off her plight. This caused problems.

"It is not allowed. The hospital cannot take responsibility. All the other patients might want to do the same thing," I was told.

I pointed out that it would not be necessary if the hospital radio was properly serviced to receive all the programmes it was supposed to. Eventually I agreed to sign a paper absolving the hospital from responsibility and left my mother happily listening to the Archers. I had been in the north-west a week.

I spent the next week in London. Frank arrived back from America and we spent all our evenings together. During the day I was plunged back into the world of work, of appointments and deadlines while my evenings were immersed in talk of boats and the future. My anxieties for my mother faded as each day the ward staff reported her improvement.

On Friday 18 October, I left London on the train at lunch-time. I caught the number 12 bus to the hospital. My mother was lying on her bed. Both eyes were closed again. She was lethargic with no idea what day it was or what was going on. Jill and Alison arrived and also another neighbour, but my mother took little interest. We left the hospital together, both of them saying how ill she looked.

I went back in the evening, brought some food and fed her. She ate quite well and asked me to help her to the lavatory. As I held her, I realised how much weight she had lost. I found she could hardly walk and it was a struggle to make the short distance there and back. She fell back on the bed exhausted. My body ached with fear and wretchedness.

"Would you like me to read your Bible?" I asked.

"Yes," she said, "Psalm 23."

I found the place, my throat tight and aching I began, "The Lord is my shepherd: I shall not want. He maketh me to lie down in green pastures . . . ."

The tears welled up. I struggled on. She put out her hand to me. I laid my head on her bed and wept bitterly.

"Don't be upset," she said. "I have no fear. God is with me. He has pulled me through worse things than this. It will be all right. You'll see."

She stroked my hair, comforting me; the tears began to dry. As a child I knew that, if she said it would be all right, then it was. I was her child again and I left the hospital with hope in my heart.

It was short lived. Next day I found her, eyes closed, sitting in an armchair by her bed. She was confused, talking in broken sentences. Yesterday's strength had ebbed away. I wanted to gather her up in my arms and take her out of this place. She needed peace and quiet, and rest. She needed good food and loving care. I wanted her out of this dingy, noisy ward with its peeling paint, blaring television, squeeling trolleys and bright fluorescent lights. I wanted her away from these hard-faced Mother Gamps who pretended to be nurses. I wanted her home in her own bed. I wanted to look after her, to take care of her and to make her better.

It was Sunday. I ought to be going back to London. Instead, I went back to my mother's house and telephoned Alison. As editor of Britain's largest nursing journal, she was horrified at the tale of my mother's care. She had a journal to produce but she also practised the caring principles the journal advocated.

"You must stay there," she said. "I will have your work sent up. Cancel your appointments and we'll sort out the time owing later. Whatever happens, stop worrying."

I put the phone down, feeling happier.

I rang Frank and told him I was going to try to get my mother home tomorrow. I did not want to discharge her against medical advice; so I had arranged to see the consultant after his round.

Frank agreed that this seemed like the best solution and offered to drive the car up for me—I would need it.

This time the consultant had his junior doctors and the ward sister with him.

"We've done everything we can," he said, "but we cannot find out what is wrong."

I wondered whether he knew of the muddles over drugs, the missed meals and drinks, the ambulance trip to the eye clinic and that the infected right eye was almost certainly caused by bad nursing practice.

"You may have done what you can," I said, "but in the meantime she is deteriorating badly and she is confused."

"Confused?" he queried. "Sister, have you noticed that she is confused?"

"No," the sister said, "she's perfectly all right."

I felt like saying, "She'd need to be stark staring mad for sister and her band of nurses to notice anything."

Instead I said, "I'd really like to take her home."

The consultant was enthusiastic.

"It might help to get her away from the hospital. She may be depressed. I did wonder about calling in the psychiatrist—anti-depressants might be the answer."

My mother would have been horrified. She had no time for psychiatrists or their anti-depressants.

"Depression," she would say. "Nonsense. Stop thinking about yourself. Find some hard work and a few others worse off than you."

I felt oddly amused that they should be so far wrong about the kind of person my mother was and that they seemed unaware that their care made people ill. They provided not even one of the first healing essentials—rest, peace, good food, fresh air and loving care.

"No," I replied, "let me try first."

"All right," he said, "take her home tomorrow and bring her back to the ward for my round on Thursday."

There was much to be done. I went back into the ward and told her I would take her home the next morning. I hurried back to the house to get the heating going and some food in. I rang Frank in London who said he would bring the car straight away. Now I had a new set of worries. Frank had never visited my mother's house before. I wanted him to come but how was I to explain

12

him to my mother? I had no wish to add to her troubles. I worked myself into a state of nervous tension as I dashed about collecting clothes, airing sheets, shopping and rushing to the hospital to feed her. By the time Frank arrived, I was exhausted.

We arrived on the ward at 9 am. She was sitting in an armchair by her bed, leaning forwards. As I walked up the ward, I knew she was listening like a blind person for my footsteps. My eyes filled with tears. Eight weeks before, she had walked into the hospital carrying her own suitcase. She was going home too weak to walk unaided, mentally confused, emaciated, temporarily blind, her face covered in black scabs and in severe pain. The only real treatment she had received was a blood transfusion for anaemia.

We borrowed a wheelchair from the ward and sister gave me her drugs. We managed to get her into the car, and Frank and I between us half carried her into the house and helped her to a chair in the sitting room. I suggested making coffee.

"Could I have something to eat?" she asked. "I asked the staff nurse to help me with my porridge but she must have forgotten. I had no breakfast."

I boiled her an egg which she ate with some bread and butter. She had not slept well and wanted to go to bed. It took both Frank and I to get her up the stairs. She slept for most of the day. I woke her two-hourly to instil the eye drops.

"Why so often?" she asked.

"You're supposed to have them two-hourly," I replied.

"It was only three times a day in the hospital," she told me.

It was hardly surprising her eyes had not healed in the three weeks as expected.

The next day she was much improved. I gave her breakfast in bed and she came downstairs in her dressing-gown. She walked with the help of one person and could see a little. She and Frank chatted while I served lunch. She still could not feed herself properly as she seemed unable to synchronise a spoon with her mouth. I noticed the same loss of co-ordination later when I would have expected her to be able to instil her own eye drops but she could not.

We had just finished lunch when, to my horror, Frank suddenly said, "What Wendy and I really want from you is your blessing."

13

I sat rigid, transfixed. Had he asked me, I would never have agreed to this. What new disaster was upon me?

My mother seemed unperturbed. She said she had suspected for a long time and she appreciated his directness. She asked Frank about his marriage and told him something of her own unhappy experience.

"I'm in no position to judge others," she told him. "All I want is Wendy's happiness."

He asked whether he might stay another day and come back again.

"By all means," she said, "you are welcome."

This climax of nervous tension was too much for me. I wept copiously and it took both of them to calm me. When I finally recovered, my head ached but I felt happy. I remember it as one of the happiest evenings of my life. We sat round the fire in her small cosy sitting room while Frank read aloud to my mother from one of his books.

The next day was Thursday—the day of the consultant's ward round. We were up early and my mother managed to wash and dress. Her clothes hung loosely round her—even her shoes semed big. It was a cold stormy day and it was difficult to protect her tender painful face against the piercing wind. I dreaded going near the ward. What if the consultant wanted to take her in again? In two days she had changed. She was still weak but she could see a little and she had regained her dignity and bearings. The tottering geriatric look had gone.

I was perspiring with panic by the time we reached the ward. We were assailed by the same dusty corridor dotted with fire buckets filled with cigarette ends, the same smell of stale cabbage and pea, and the same bustle and bright lights.

"She'll have to be examined here," said the nurse, showing us to another patient's bed and drawing the curtains.

"Undress and lie on the bed for the doctor to examine you," she told my mother.

"Do you think we could have a clean sheet to cover the bed?" I asked, eyeing the dirty bed apprehensively.

We were given a clean sheet but it was typical of the lack of care for cross-infection or cleanliness.

The consultant was delighted with my mother's progress.

"Keep up the good work," he said, "but bring her back next

week. Who would have believed it—a case of hospitalitis in a retired ward sister."

I said nothing. I wanted to get out of this hell-hole and home to my mother's house.

I took Frank to the bus for London after lunch. Then both my mother and I lay on our beds and slept—both of us exhausted. Later we had supper and sat mulling over the events of the last few days late into the night.

I could not stay any longer but my mother needed looking after. I rang Aunt Emily. She was my mother's younger sister by eight years. They had always been close friends and visited each other every year. Aunt Emily, a farmer's widow, lived in Ireland in a cottage on the farm now owned by her son—my cousin Harry.

Aunt Emily arrived a week later. I drove to Liverpool in the early morning to meet the Dublin ferry. It was a chill grey morning and the seagulls shrieked and twirled over the water as I watched the ferry dock. The crowds poured off into the covered gangway, disappeared into the customs shed, to emerge in small bewildered batches. Aunt Emily, short and stocky with no trace of grey in her flaming red hair, plodded off last. I hugged her. Safe, secure Aunt Emily, a part of those long-ago days of sunshine and harvesting. I caught the bus for London in the afternoon.

Aunt Emily stayed six weeks. She kept house and cooked good plain Irish meals. She instilled the eye drops, chatted to the neighbours, entertained the visitors, kept my mother company and knitted a large green Aran jumper.

My mother thrived. She ate well and put on a little weight. She needed few pain killers and no sleeping tablets. The infection in the right eye cleared up and the left eye improved. Bit by bit the black scabs peeled off. At first she had needed a bell at night as she could not find her way to the lavatory next door to her room—her sense of direction gone. Under Aunt Emily's regime, it returned. Her strength grew and she began to tackle small jobs in the house.

I was back at work in London but travelled the two hundred miles north every other weekend. I did the heavy shopping and relished the warmth and happiness in the house as my mother improved and she and Aunt Emily enjoyed each other's company. I wished that Aunt Emily could stay forever.

15

We talked a lot.

"I'd have died in that hospital if you hadn't taken me out. I know I would," my mother told us.

"Why don't you let me make a formal complaint?," I urged. "Something ought to be done about that place. It's a disgrace. I'll take it to the health service ombudsman if I have to."

"I've worked in the place for years," my mother said. "Complaints cause bad feeling and no improvements. It's my local hospital. I may have to go in there again—there's nowhere else to go. I know you mean well but I'll have to suffer the consequences. Promise me you won't complain."

Reluctantly I promised. Deep down I knew that, despite clear complaints procedures and government directives, in practice my mother was right. Complaints were fine when you were dead or moved away but not while still a patient.

"You'll never have to go in there again if I can help it," I declared defiantly.

At *Nursing Times*, Alison tried to persuade me to write about the experience.

"It's unbelievable," she said. "You should write about it— please try."

I could not. I wrote furiously in my journal almost every day. Minute details mixed with wrathful outpourings—a release of anger but it was not for publication. It was vicious and destructive. I could see no other side to the story. I could find no excuses. I could not believe that the staff might know no better—products of poor practice stretching incestuously back to the workhouse the hospital once was. I could not see that the staff were as much the victims of bad management as the patients. It is only now that I begin to see it in perspective.

Although my mother was on the mend, the problem of anaemia had still to be solved. We were only starting to get back to where we had been in August. I began to see the impossibility of the dreams that Frank and I had dreamed together. He might have asked for my mother's blessing but now he might not want me, shackled with a dependant. I pushed the idea to the back of my mind—after all it might never happen and next year was far into the future.

Aunt Emily wanted to get home to prepare for Christmas. My mother still needed some help and I suggested we might be able to get a home help and meals-on-wheels. I rang the local authority social services department and the home help organiser came to visit. She arranged for my mother to have a home help three mornings weekly and meals-on-wheels would be delivered daily. I would come at weekends.

My mother still could not manage her eye drops which were now four-hourly. I asked the district nurse to help.

"No, you'll have to make your own arrangements. We cannot visit four-hourly," was all they had to offer.

We had no solution. It seemed too much to ask of a neighbour. Finally we rang the family doctor. He changed the prescription to twice daily and asked the district nurses to administer them. In the end, my mother stopped this arrangement and her next-door neighbour took it on. The nurses came late at night when my mother was tired and needed to sleep. Living alone, she was also reluctant to open the door after dark.

Before Aunt Emily left, she addressed all the Christmas cards as my mother still could not see well enough to write legibly. They parted tearfully, not wanting to say goodbye. Still there was only a week before I would be at home with her for Christmas.

Christmas 1980 was one of the happiest I remember. Shortly before Christmas I arrived late in the evening to find my mother flushed and busy in the kitchen. Apple tarts, mince pies and cakes were being produced. While most of the black scabs had gone, her eye still watered continuously, making it difficult for her to cook. I chided her for working so hard. She laughed. She was happy. If she wanted to do it, why should I stop her?

Over Christmas a steady stream of visitors popped in. Coffee and mince pies were continuous. The house was warm and happy, festooned with cards, holly and flowers. My mother enjoyed herself talking to old friends and getting better all the time.

One evening sitting by the fire I asked her about the future. What would she want to do if the day came that she could not manage alone anymore.

"I'm better now," she said. "I'll be all right to live here for some time yet."

She loved her house and garden. It had been hard won and she wanted to stay there. I was still unsure of my future—whether it lay with Frank or not and, if it did, where we would live and what we would do.

"Would you live with Frank and me if we had a home?" I asked.

"If I could no longer live here, then I would like to live with you, provided that Frank was agreeable and I could pay my way," she said.

She lived on a shoestring but would never agree to any arrangement she could not afford. She dismissed the idea of being dependent as being far into the future and we changed the subject.

Frank arrived for New Year—his birthday. My mother was now in charge and running her own house again and Frank had to have the full visitor treatment—family silver, enormous meals and flowers in his room. She could not be dissuaded from it. On New Year's Eve we joined in Mrs Brereton's happy family party next door. We sang 'Auld lang syne' at midnight and half an hour later in my mother's sitting room the three of us raised our glasses to 1981 and a Happy New Year.

We left on 4 January. It was bitterly cold. Flakes of snow drifted across the front door as I ran back to close the garden gate. She stood in the doorway, smiling hesitantly. I remember her green skirt hung loosely, betraying her loss of weight. I looked up and she stretched out her arms to me. I ran up the steps and we hugged each other.

"Take care," she said. "Don't worry. I'm fine now."

I wanted to stay, to take care of her and to stop going to London but I turned away, heart heavy and eyes burning. After all I would see her again in two weeks—she was better now.

2 First Encounter

Frank writes up to December 1980

I first met her at the flat in London when Wendy and I had been together for two years. I was made to move out to make room for her—the flat was tiny, two rooms, bathroom and a diminutive kitchen. I went the day before she arrived; all traces of my occupation of the flat were tidied away, my few clothes bundled into an old suitcase, my toothbrush secreted in the bathroom cupboard and my seaboots stuffed under the bed. My books were relegated to a top back shelf and out I went.

The next day at the appointed time I ascended in the lift and rang the bell with trepidation. Wendy opened the door and I saw Adeline sitting on the settee by the French windows to the balcony. She was a little woman, and she sat very erect and compact; she looked young for her seventy-four years. She shook my hand with a firm grip; her pale, grey eyes bored into me, instantly revealing my secrets, my private deceptions. She spoke with an Irish brogue, a little broader than Wendy's. Her skin was white and clear, and her hair grey, touched with auburn. This meeting was a major hurdle in Wendy's and my affair, which had known many.

Adeline lived in the north of England. Wendy would drive up to see her in the Mini every few weeks and occasionally, once or twice a year, her mother would come to London for a few days. She liked to look at the shops, she took a proprietary interest in the flat and Wendy would take her to the theatre or the ballet. They slept side by side in Wendy's double bed. At first, I was banished altogether during these visits but later, when our relationship had settled down, it was agreed that I should meet Adeline.

It was no hardship for me to leave the flat for a night or two because my boat *Iskra* was lying at that time in St Katherine's dock, not far away from the flat. She was there because one of my books about her had just been published and I was to invite various worthies from the book trade on board for drinks—a kind of small-scale publicity stunt. Sailing and writing about sailing were and are a large part of my life, a part of my life that Wendy joins in. For the past two summers, Wendy had spent her holidays sailing with me. We had sailed up the east coast of England together and down to the Channel Islands. Now I was about to sail *Iskra* across the Atlantic. My first stop would be the Azores, and Wendy was going to fly out and spend part of her summer holiday with me before I set out for America.

I wanted Wendy to tell Adeline that we were living together before I went away but she was reluctant—perhaps she still was not quite sure that we would endure together. I was not free to marry her. Even if I had been, at that time neither of us thought much of the idea. I believe Wendy was frightened of Adeline— frightened of her opinion, her sharp tongue and her disapproval. Wendy was her only surviving child out of three; her brothers both died, one at birth and the other when six months old. Adeline was possessive towards her only child.

Adeline bore the psychological scars of an unhappy and frustrated life. She had trained as a nurse at the Royal City of Dublin Hospital in the 1920s and, after a few years, had gone to work in Torquay where she met and married Wendy's father. It was not a success. He was a businessman, running a thriving nursing agency, but he was also a heavy drinker who later became an alcoholic. Adeline was accepted into the prosperous Torquay society of which Wendy's father was a part. The first few years of her married life, apart from her two unlucky pregnancies, were the happiest. Then it all came to a sudden end. When Adeline returned from the hospital, Wendy in her arms, she found another woman living in her home. Three months later, she gathered up her child, left Torquay with her few possessions and went back to Ireland.

Adeline found she was not welcomed by her own mother. Wendy's grandmother, whom Wendy remembers well, at first would not have her in the house. She was a martinet with a narrow, puritanical outlook—Wendy's family are Irish protestants. According to her interpretation, Adeline had behaved stupidly if not sinfully in leaving her husband, whatever cause. It was only on the intercession of Adelir[e]'s father, a less forceful character than his spouse but having a streak of compassion that made him rise against her tyranny towards his daughter, that Adeline was accepted back and came home to Knockboy, the farm in County Carlow where Wendy was brought up.

Soon after Adeline and Wendy returned to Knockboy, Adeline's mother broke her hip and was then smitten with a stroke. This was soon followed by another and she became an invalid. It was on Adeline, the only unattached one of three sisters, that the job of looking after her mother fell. The arrangement started when Adeline was forty years old and continued until she was fifty-two years old. She spent twelve years of her life caring for an old lady who was always difficult and perverse, who was often intractable and who took no trouble to disguise the feelings of contempt she held for her daughter.

Adeline was paid no salary for her work; her family considered that board and lodging for herself and Wendy was sufficient reward for looking after an invalid and running the farmhouse. When the maid left and could not be replaced, Adeline demanded and was given her salary. She had a pittance of maintenance from her husband, whom she refused to divorce— she kept chickens to earn a few shillings, and she saved every penny she had to give Wendy an education. Wendy grew up on the farm, going to school in Rathvilly some three miles distant from Knockboy. She walked to the village and made the rest of the journey in a donkey cart with the Mackenna family. Later she rode a bicycle. Wendy won a scholarship to a boarding school in County Kildare where she remained until she started her nurse training at the Royal Victoria Hospital in Belfast.

When Wendy's grandmother died, Adeline's brother, who had inherited the farm, refused to make any provision for her or to give her any financial security. Fearing that he might marry and render her pennyless and homeless, she decided to leave Knockboy and to go back to work. She took the ferry to England and got a job as a nurse at a nearby hospital. She soon became a ward sister in charge of the geriatric ward. With the pennies she had skimped and saved, she bought a house—just round the corner from the hospital. It is a good house, chosen with Adeline's sharp eye for value. It stands on a corner, it has a marginally larger garden than its fellows, and it has a garage which Adeline was able to let for £1 per week.

It is hard to understand why Adeline chose this particular town as home for herself and Wendy for the rest of her life—there are other more salubrious areas in which to live and she had no one to please but herself. It had an element of convenience about it; as long as Wendy was at the Royal Victoria Hospital, it was not far from the north of Ireland, but it is a gloomy place. The hospital was originally built as a workhouse in the middle of the last century and converted to a hospital just before the war. It is a gaunt, gloomy place of dark stone with the sure stamp of nineteenth-century sanctimony upon it. Its stone staircases, high narrow windows and echoing corridors still smell of the poor laws.

Adeline had become deeply, even fanatically religious—the move to the north of England may have been something in the nature of a penance. She became abstemious of everything that could be construed as vice, every self-indulgence and every vain pleasure. She went to church on Sunday, she took part in church activities and she conducted her life with a fierce economy, saving every penny and denying herself holidays, treats and luxuries. She knew she would get no proper pension because her stamp had never been paid for all the time she worked at Knockboy. Her pride would never have allowed her to take social security. Refusing to divorce her husband, she divorced herself from her past, her gay life in Torquay. She would have nothing to do with any of her relations by marriage, who in fact harboured only goodwill towards her. She denied Wendy all knowledge of her father and her aunts, uncles and cousins on her father's side.

As far as Wendy was concerned, she might never have had a father—he died when Wendy was eight years old. He wanted to see Wendy before he died but Adeline refused, saying that she did not have the money for the return fare from Ireland to Torquay. Wendy never saw her father after the age of three months. Adeline's choice of home town and of that hospital as a workplace must have been a kind of punishment directed at herself, a mortification, a flagellation as a religious discipline.

Wendy had scant sympathy for her mother's religious fervour. She tolerated it but was not prepared to take it as a pattern for her own life. While she was engaged in her nursing training, she spent her brief holidays at her mother's home more out of a sense of duty towards her mother than for the pleasure and enjoyment the place offered. It is not an exciting spot. The house was pleasant enough—comfortable and adequately, although inexpensively, furnished according to Adeline's taste. Adeline lavished on the garden what spare time and energy she had left over from the hospital. The house is surrounded by an ocean of semi-detached houses much like it, inhabited by people whom Adeline did not relate to, with some exceptions, and with whom Wendy found no points of contact.

Adeline lavished on the garden what spare time she had left over from the hospital

Not surprisingly, when Wendy qualified as a nurse, she sought her fortunes elsewhere. She worked in a large town nearby as a midwife for a spell and tried to live at her mother's home but found it impossible. She loved her mother but could not tolerate interference in her personal affairs and the air of disapproval that her mother laid on her. The religious aspect was overpowering. She went to London, qualified as a health visitor and gravitated to a flat in Chelsea where she lived a happy, higgledy-piggledy life with people of her own age and outlook who shared her sentiments. When I met her, she had her own flat, a responsible job in the NHS and, although she did not know it, she was tentatively taking the first steps towards making herself into a writer.

It was easy to see that Wendy had the outlook on life and a flair for unearthing what is amusing and at the same time important to make her into a journalist. She had written a book about school nursing, which was at that time her speciality and she had started to write articles for nursing journals. The first day I met her, after a long lunch-time's talk, I went and bought her book to read— she also wanted to read mine except that, instead of buying them, she went to the library and borrowed them, thus illustrating one of the differences between us. When I met her, she had recently been to Japan to a nursing conference where she met the then Editor of the *Nursing Times*, Alison Dunne, who asked her to write a number of articles for the magazine. A year later, Alison offered her a job and I encouraged her to take it—to give up the safety of her career in the NHS and to cast herself into the jungle of competitive journalism. I began to help her with her writing, as she helped me with mine. She took to the excitements and the intellectual stimulus of the profession and soon carved herself a niche in the world of nursing journalism. I have taken a vicarious pleasure in her success.

At the beginning, Wendy and I did not have an easy ride in forming our relationship and Adeline's attitude towards our affair made it no easier. Like most mothers, Adeline wanted Wendy to settle down and marry some nice respectable man, to live in a nice respectable house and to bring up a nice respectable family. So far, Wendy had shown no inclination whatsoever in this direction. Before she met me, her male friends, at least those that Adeline knew anything about, had been for the most part highly unsuitable. They were already married or had no intention of getting married, at least not to Wendy, or Wendy herself had rejected them. Adeline disapproved completely and registered her disapproval in the clearest terms. I was no better in her eyes than my predecessors. I was already married; for good measure, I had been married twice and Adeline saw no prospect of me fulfilling the role she had mapped out in her mind for her son-in-law. She saw no prospect of anything good coming out of an association between Wendy and me.

At first, Wendy herself was half inclined to agree with her mother. She had been in many respects badly used by the men in her life and she had been left by them with her hackles raised and her defences bristling with barbed spears. It took many weeks and months of patient work for me to break down her resistance, to instil in her a modicum of trust and to persuade her that my intentions were honourable. The difference between myself and the others was that I really loved her but it took Wendy a long time to understand this, to me, very simple truth and longer still for her to respond to it with a like feeling.

For me, Wendy was my last chance to salvage my life from a state of hopeless confusion and unhappiness. I met her when I was almost at the end of my tether and in desperate straights. The affair started shakily. We got on well, shared the same sense of humour and were happy when we were together but Wendy was determined not to allow herself to become involved with someone who was already married—she had been bitten too often in the past. However, she found it difficult to get rid of me because we were happy and carefree, like young lovers, when we were together. I kept bouncing back at her each time she threw me out, like a rubber ball. The first summer we went sailing together, I knew that we had hit on something permanent. To be in *Iskra* together was to be exposed to an infectious happiness neither of us cared to resist. Wendy came to Guernsey in the early summer where I had taken the boat to a book fair where my publisher was exhibiting.

The first time she saw *Iskra* was from the top of the marina gangway, smart in new paint and shining varnish, lying alongside the pontoon with her usual welcoming, homely aspect. We went on board; Wendy climbed down through the hatch into *Iskra*'s saloon and looked around her at the varnished wood, the chart table, the brass cabin lamps, the clock and barometer side by side on a wooden plaque, the cosy berths, the neat galley, the books in shelves round the ship's side, my sextant in its box, the compass on the bulkhead, and the mug of wild flowers I had put there for her—all the trappings of a way of life I wanted her to share with me. She fell for it head over heels. She did not know she had fallen for it and for me, but I knew it—from the moment she saw *Iskra*, it was only a matter of time before she fell for us both, me and *Iskra*, which she soon did.

Adeline was spry and well the day I first saw her in the flat. As she got up from the settee when I came in to the room and we shook hands, the thought flashed across my mind that this is what Wendy will look like at the same age. Her eyes were full of fun, her movements quick and incisive. She had none of the slow understanding that often goes with age. She was well informed, read the newspaper every day and followed the Stock Market, caring for her tiny investments. She had strong opinions on many topics and voiced them with an air of certitude. For the most part they were not of the political shade I could share with her. Her stance was well to the right of almost everything but, when challenged, she was never dismissive of an opposing view. She would take a point and give a point but would not allow herself to be shaken from her convictions.

We had an amusing, and Wendy thought a successful, dinner party in the flat—before I left, I asked Adeline and Wendy on board *Iskra* the next evening. They came to St Katherine's dock and *Iskra* cast her spell on Adeline just as she had on Wendy. Although she was still vehemently disapproving, Adeline had softened by the time we had met and conversed. I believe she regarded me as an immoral influence on her daughter but possibly as the best of a bad lot among Wendy's boy-friends. She liked the neatness and good order she found on board *Iskra*.

In the spring of 1980, Wendy and I sailed *Iskra* round the coast of England from Maldon, in the River Blackwater in Essex to Dartmouth. We sailed at weekends from port to port along the south coast. I made the last passage by myself, from the Hamble river to Dartmouth where Wendy came for a last weekend before I set off for the Azores. She helped me to buy the last of *Iskra*'s stores and to get ready for the thousand-odd mile leg to Ponta Delgada. Apart from stores, *Iskra* was full of my books which I hoped to sell in America to pay for the voyage. They were packed in parcels of twenty copies, each wrapped in polythene and the seams taped over to keep them dry—four hundred copies of

Schooner Integrity and four hundred copies of a novel I had written two years previously, called *Rustler on the Beach*. I hoped to sell the books and at the same time to find a publisher for *Schooner Integrity* in America. To help Wendy's peace of mind, I had bought *Iskra* a VHF radio so that I could send messages to any ship I came across in the ocean to be relayed to my office in London and thence to Wendy.

The voyage to America went pretty well as Wendy and I had planned it. Wendy came to Ponta Delgaga and we spent ten days together, exploring the island and discovering its many attractions. We spent hours walking round the little town together, we hired a car to discover the wild interior and all the time we lived on board *Iskra* anchored in the harbour. The sun shone and it was beautiful. We busied ourselves preparing *Iskra* for what would be the most difficult voyage I had ever made—across the Atlantic from east to west against the prevailing westerly winds. It was a long and tedious voyage, even unpleasant and dangerous at times. I was thirty-four days by myself in the ocean and arrived in Newport with less than a week in hand before Wendy came out by plane. When she arrived she showed me a letter from Adeline that had arrived at the flat before she left—the hurt of it was plain to see in her eyes.

"I hate and detest and deplore this visit to Frank," Adeline wrote.

Wendy came out for two weeks and we cruised around Long Island Sound and Buzzard's Bay before she flew back to England. It was a care-free, idyllic time—the last holiday free from worry we were to have for years. We both love the life we lead in the boat—a casual progress from one place to the next, getting to know new people and discovering a new country. I found no difficulty in selling the books—the Americans loved them and bought them so fast that I began to run out. Book money paid for the whole holiday.

We were full of plans for the future. We would try to organise our lives so that we could both go off on board *Iskra*. I would concentrate more on my writing and less on my business so that I would soon be able to pass the business over to someone else and earn my living by my pen. Wendy would work up a good freelance connection in addition to her work on *Nursing Times* so that, wherever we went, we would be able to earn the modest amount which is sufficient to keep us on board the boat. We

27

would let the flat in London and the income, together with our bits and pieces of writing, would keep us off the breadline. Once our commitments were taken care of, we would only have ourselves to please and, with *Iskra*, the world would be our oyster.

If we wanted to, Wendy and I could take *Iskra* to any part of the world we chose. The future was rosy. Both of us, for the first time in our lives, had resolved our emotional puzzles to our satisfaction. We were full of happiness, full of plans and full of bright imaginings. We decided to leave *Iskra* in America for the winter and to come back to her the following summer. Wendy flew home and I stayed on for a few weeks, found a good boat yard in Providence where *Iskra* would be safe, tucked her up snug and warm under an old tarpaulin and followed Wendy home.

When I got back to the flat, Adeline was ill and Wendy had gone north to be near her. I read the brief note Wendy left for me and looked round the empty flat. For the first time, it occurred to me that life was not going to be quite as straightforward and rosy as I had imagined.

"Bloody bigoted old woman," I muttered to myself.

3 Stroke

Wendy writes January–March 1981

On 14 January, my mother had a stroke. Frank and I drove through the night, the blizzard blinding us with sleet and snow.

"A small stroke," someone from the hospital had said, "she hasn't spoken. Yes, perhaps you ought to come."

We arrived at 2 am but the night nurse said she was asleep.

"Come back in the morning," she told us.

At 9 am we arrived at the hospital—the same ward we knew so well. At first I could not find her among the long rows of beds. Then I saw her wrapped in a hospital dressing-gown slumped in a chair, a pool of urine on the floor. I knelt beside her and hugged her. She did not seem to know me. I crouched beside her, hopelessly defeated, unable even to shield her indignity from public gaze—my mother, so fastidious, so careful of her appearance, so proud and so self-sufficient. I sat with her all day. Sister brought me a cup of tea.

"I'm sorry," she said, reaching out to me.

I stared back at her, numbly. Frank brought me lunch. I sat there. I felt nothing, heard nothing and thought nothing. I just sat there.

I stayed a week. Like a robot, I walked to and fro to the hospital at lunch-time and supper-time to help her with her food. I rang Aunt Emily. I wrote to Aunt Alice—my mother's other sister living in the north of Ireland. I talked to Alison at *Nursing Times*. I did no work. I sat silently in my mother's bedroom in her house. I moved aimlessly about the house, touching things as she left them, moving nothing and not wanting to destroy the last vestiges of the person she had been.

29

I began to reproach myself. Why had I done nothing? When I had telephoned her, she had told me she did not feel well. She had pains in her legs. I noticed her voice was slow. When I rang the consultant, he told me he feared she might be heading for a stroke—I had done nothing. I had dismissed it, hoping it would go away. I had made up my mind my mother was better and I was irritated by signs that it might not be true. I wanted to get back to my previous way of life. I hated my erratic working pattern—it embarrassed me. My employer and my colleagues might rally at the first emergency but would soon tire of constant special requests.

I began to think my mother had done it on purpose. Whatever she may have said, perhaps she still disapproved of Frank. If she could get rid of him no other way, her helplessness would drive him away. I wept and wept until I was sick and retching. I slept fitfully, ate badly and lost weight. I could plan nothing. There was no future. I tore and worried at what might have been. I sat helplessly waiting for events to overtake me.

I still believe that, had I responded to all the warning signals and been with her, the stroke might not have been so damaging and the next five years of our lives would have been different. She must have known what was happening for some days prior to the stroke. She must have been fearful and anxious, particularly as the shingles episode had made her frightened of the hospital. Had she been able to rest without fear or worry, things might have turned out differently. With hindsight, all of us would act differently I suppose.

A stroke happens when the blood supply to some of the brain cells is impaired, usually by a clot of blood or haemorrhage. The effects depend on which part of the brain is damaged, the extent of the damage and for how long the circulation is cut off. It is possible to recover completely from a brief stoppage but a large one usually ends in permanent damage or death. My mother had lost the use of her right side—her right arm and hand and her right leg. The sight of her right eye which had not been damaged by the shingles was restricted. A right-sided stroke follows damage to the left side of the brain which controls speech; therefore, speech, reading and writing may also be affected. Many words no longer have any meaning. Conversation is not understood or only partially comprehended, nor can the victim form a reply. Often a jumble of meaningless words emerge and stroke victims frequently indicate no when they mean yes. My mother lost not only her speech but also her ability to read and write.

I can only guess what she must have felt. Those who have recovered have described the bewildering isolation, locked inside half a body—one side dead, no longer felt or even recognised as belonging. Strange faces flit about.

"Do I know her? She seems familiar."

The face asks, "Do —— a ——?"

"What can she mean? What is the cart of dishes she is wheeling? Is she asking if I'd like a drink? Yes, that must be it. Yes, I'd like a cup of tea. Why is my head shaking when I mean to nod? Oh! I do want tea—why is she pushing the cart away?"

The frustration mounts as the victim tries to make sense of a bewildering world. Asking for something and trying to find ways of being understood is daunting. Friends, relatives and hospital staff are uncomprehending, not knowing what is wanted or whether the patient is saying yes or no. If reading and writing are also affected, the patient is totally isolated. Some words may be recognised but the meaning not understood.

For example, if you show the victim a list and ask, "Which is the word cup?", the patient may recognise it but, if you then ask, "Which of these dishes is a cup?" the patient may pick up a saucer.

Intense frustration can manifest itself in anger, tears, violence or hysteria. To begin with most patients are emotional—one moment depressed or weeping and the next gabbling and laughing excitedly.

When my mother had her stroke, I knew none of this. Although I qualified as a general nurse, I cannot remember ever nursing a stroke patient. It seems hardly credible that such a common illness (about 100 000 cases yearly in the UK) was not part of my experience but, if it was, I do not remember it. Most of my career had been spent with mothers and children, and clinical nursing was not part of my job at *Nursing Times*. I was as unaware of the care and treatment my mother needed as any other relative, in spite of being a trained nurse.

Like many of the other relatives visiting this ward, I desperately needed information and guidance—there was none. The nurses told us nothing. I believe that most of them knew little more than we did ourselves. Learner nurses came and went through this ward little wiser for their experience. With other relatives, I spent hours sitting in the corridor, waiting for doctors' rounds to end or for the ward to be opened. We knew the 'No Smoking' sign by heart and the instructions on how to operate the anaesthetic machine which shared our space. Although perhaps half of the twenty-four or so patients on the ward had strokes of one kind or another, there were no leaflets to explain the nature of a stroke—what it is, how best to respond to it and how to help the patient. There was not even a notice or poster giving addresses such as that of the Chest, Heart and Stroke Association, from which to seek advice.

Sitting in the dingy corridor, I often thought of the Margaret Pyke Family Planning Centre in London, its waiting room festooned with explanatory leaflets on contraception. Samples of useful books on sale are displayed and there is usually a video featuring the Director of the Centre explaining the latest findings on the pill.

I imagined this drab corridor transformed—a lick of paint, an attractive leaflet display, and the anaesthetic machine replaced by a video showing us how to talk to our relatives and encourage their independence. It would have been money well invested— patients would go home sooner and be less likely to be readmitted because their relatives could not cope. It would not be difficult to test the truth of this.

I was luckier than other relatives as I knew how and where to find information. I use medical libraries constantly as part of my work and I am familiar with the ramifications of health and social services, but seeking information is time consuming. I was trying to keep in touch with my mother, to do a full-time job, to commute between London and my mother's home town two hundred miles away and to run two homes with all the complications of bills and problems that my mother's inability to read or write were causing. Over the weeks to come, I visited the Chest, Heart and Stroke Association and telephoned several organisations for leaflets and help. I visited libraries and ransacked *Nursing Times* office for relevant books. When I finally knew enough to be of real help to my mother, the time when it would have been most effective was past.

For the fullest possible recovery, intensive therapy must start right away. The speech therapist, physiotherapist and occupational therapist each need to assess the patient's abilities and to work out a comprehensive plan of therapy. If my mother's ward had been well managed, each patient would have had a plan of care. The plan for my mother would have included the nursing care she needed as well as what the therapists aimed to do. The social worker would have been involved and I would have been asked to contribute as much information as possible about my mother's likes, dislikes, recreations and interests. The staff would have used this to arrange her care around what she would be most likely to respond to. The aim would be to get my mother to use her remaining abilities as fast as possible so that she might regain some independence and quality of life. The plan would start with small goals to be achieved day by day. The staff would have worked together to complement each other's achievements and to teach relatives or friends so that they too could help.

With such a plan the staff would have known that my mother had always been addressed as Mrs Slack except by relatives and close friends who called her Adeline. They would not have persisted in calling her by her first name, Sarah, which must have added to her confusion. When the physiotherapists tried to get her walking with a tripod and to move from bed to chair with the help of one person, the nurses would have done likewise if there had been a care plan. Instead, two nurses lifted her in and out of bed and moved her about in a wheelchair. She had no opportunity to improve her skills between one physiotherapy session and the next. The constant changing of methods of lifting and moving must have slowed her progress.

On the second day following my mother's stroke, I arrived on the ward to find the physiotherapists trying to get my mother to walk. Suspended between two of them, she looked like a collapsed bundle of clothes. Her head drooped and her legs crumpled beneath her. I watched from the ward door, feeling hopeless. What would become of us? I wondered.

"Head up," urged the physiotherapists. "Now, foot forward. No, no—like this."

On and on they went. I marvelled at their persistence. In the afternoon they took her to the physiotherapy department for arm and hand exercises. The pattern of their programme was set.

When not being encouraged, dragooned and cajoled by the ever-optimistic physiotherapists, she sat by her bed in an armchair, resting her paralysed arm on the bedtable in front of her.

She recognised me now and greeted me with an agitated "La, la, la."

I tried to encourage her.

"You look a lot better," I said. "The legs will start to work again with practice. You'll see."

"La, la, la, la," she replied.

I knew nothing about loss of speech and so I did not observe which words she seemed to understand and which she did not. I might have helped her by building on the association of words and objects. One of the staff had left a large card featuring a series of pictures of common objects such as spectacles, a cup, a bedpan and a book. She was supposed to use this to indicate her needs. I did not realise that it was useless as she understood neither the words nor the pictures. Had I known more, I could have found the objects and given her the opportunity to try to make the connection between word and object.

I continued to talk to her as though there was nothing the matter with her speech. I told her that Frank and I were staying in her house and recounted the happenings at her home. I tried to reassure her that she would get better and come home again. Most of the time I had no idea what she was trying to say to me and, if I got it right, it was by guesswork. When I was with her, she gave the impression of understanding what was being said and listened attentively and politely to me and other visitors. It was weeks before I began to have some understanding of the extent of her handicap. I often found her flushed and agitated, and the other patients told me if she had been upset. Usually, when I was with her, she seemed calm.

I wanted to see the speech therapist. I asked how and where I might contact her. Even now I do not know whether a speech therapist ever saw my mother in hospital. I asked the consultant whether she was having speech therapy and he asked sister to arrange it. When I asked him again later, he told me the speech therapist could make no headway. When five months later the family doctor referred my mother to the speech therapist, she told me she had never seen my mother at the hospital. Speech therapists are in short supply. Their training is long and their lobby in the NHS pay stakes weak. They are poorly paid and their services are low priority with some doctors and treasurers. It may be that speech therapy services were allocated to patients most likely to survive—my mother was not one of these. If this happened, it is unlikely I would be told.

Frank stayed over the weekend. He walked with me to and from the hospital and came back to fetch me. I could feel his body tense as he approached the place, and by the time we reached it his look of wretchedness was complete. In the evening, he would come into the ward, clasp my mother's hand and smile at her. One evening he handed her a bunch of snowdrops he had picked from her garden. All our eyes filled with tears.

Away from the hospital, we would walk and talk. My mother lived near some pretty country and we would drive out of the town and walk for miles. We would climb up to one of the headlands overlooking a wide estuary and gaze over the ever-changing shallow sands. We could see the mountains across the water. The wind, rain, dripping trees and green fields acted as a balm while I poured out my fears for my mother, my fury against the hospital, my worries about my job and constant re-criminations against myself. I hatched wild, hopeless plans to bundle her into the car and drive her to a London teaching hospital. Frank soothed and calmed me and pointed out the impossibility of driving my mother over two hundred miles in her present state. He had no fear—silently inside him he believed she would die.

After a week I had pulled myself together sufficiently to get back to London. I had to get on with my job. I saw Alison, told her the tale and asked whether we could work something out. She made a proposal.

"Provided that you can cope," she said, "it might be a good thing to spend some of your time based at your mother's home. Too many of our contacts are in London. We should build up more information and contacts around the country and you can make a start on Merseyside and Manchester."

I was pleased and relieved. At least for the present I could spend part of the week working from my mother's home and be near the hospital. I rang the chief nursing officer of the local health authority. She welcomed my suggestions of a feature on how nursing management was preparing for the opening of the new hospital in the coming year. I made an appointment to see her on 2 February at 2 pm. It occurred to me that this might

35

present an opportunity to discuss standards of nursing care in a friendly way.

In the meantime my mother deteriorated. Now I found her in bed and asleep when I visited the ward. She was very drowsy and difficult to rouse. For two days she lay in bed half-conscious, taking only sips of fluid. I sat by her bed, waiting for her to die. I wrote her a long rambling letter, asking her to forgive me for being so inadequate. I was miserable. There were too many loose ends between us still to be tied. I recalled my happy childhood on the farm. We were sitting together at the farmhouse table while I gossiped about the day at school and ate my dinner. We were picking primroses along the farmhouse lane. We were watching rabbits scurry into their sandpit burrows on a frosty morning. We were finding newly hatched chickens under a large white hen. It was a far cry from the north of England. On Sunday she was better. The nurses got her out of bed. She had started to recover.

The shingles episode had left me with little faith in the nursing care. Now I found it almost unbearable. I did what I could to compensate for the shortcomings and to cope with the carelessness that caused me extra work and grief. My first concern was that my mother should be fed. She ate well but she had to try to feed herself with her left hand. A plate surround was provided to stop the food falling off her plate but she could not cut the food up. She failed to see it if it was pushed to the right of her plate or the plate left on the right side of her bed table. The paralysis also affected the right side of her face and so she tended to chew on the left side and could not feel bits of food lodged in the right side of her mouth. Her co-ordination of hand and eye was poor so that she made a mess and dropped her food which upset her. At mealtimes she needed sufficient help to encourage her towards independence and at the same time to be properly nourished. The several stroke patients in the ward all suffered the same hit-and-miss regime. At one meal they were fed rather than helped to feed, and the next they were left to fend for themselves. If they had not noticed their meal or managed to finish it by the time the domestic cleared the dishes, it was thrown out. To get my mother to a stage where she could feed herself, I tried to visit at lunch- and supper-time when I could. The other patients too saw the importance of this and on a few occasions when I was late, I found that one of the more able patients had taken on the task. I was grateful for their help.

Mrs Cheers, one of my mother's neighbours, urged me on.

"Make sure you go at mealtimes," she said. "My husband, Stan, only came out of hospital because I went in and fed him every day. Don't you worry," she reassured me. "Let me know when you'll be away and I'll take over."

True to her word, Mrs Cheers, who was not well herself, faithfully turned up at my mother's bedside twice daily to help her with her food.

My mother had also lost the ability to suck. The nurses never seemed to grasp this and it caused my mother and me great distress. Patients who tended to spill their drinks had them automatically served in tall beakers with a feeding spout. To get the drink, the patient needed to be able to suck. My mother could not manage it. The drink poured out of her mouth all over her clothes but, if the top of the beaker was removed, she could drink without spilling it. I explained this, asking repeatedly if she could have a beaker without the top. No one took any notice. When I found her with a swollen cheek and a gash the shape of the beaker spout inside her mouth, I knew it had been caused by forcing a beaker into her mouth. I said so. She was examined by a doctor who said she had bitten herself. I believe this was untrue and I believe the doctor knew it was untrue. It might have helped her speech to learn to suck but, if this was the purpose of the exercise, it was cruel.

My next concern was her urinary incontinence. In common with many hospitals, provision for incontinence was primitive. I was distraught to find my mother continually lying on several sodden crumpled disposable incontinence pads of the cheapest variety. Cheap pads are a false economy. They are inefficient and so the nurses use three or four instead of one. When the patient moves, they rumple underneath, irritate the skin and cause bedsores. I often think the course for trainee health service managers should include lying in their own pee for twenty-four hours. It would revolutionise provision for incontinence in hospitals.

There are many good pads and pants on the market. The best allow the urine to pass through a one-way fabric into an absorbent pad. This is held in place by a plastic backing which protects the clothes, and provided that the pads are changed frequently, the fabric and the skin remains dry. I asked sister about these.

"I've never heard of them," she told me. "I'll ask for them but I don't hold out much hope of getting anything."

She seemed interested and I promised to bring her some leaflets.

"If I buy some Kanga pants and pads, would the nurses put them on my mother?" I asked.

"Of course," she replied helpfully.

I wondered—I still do—how could she be so ill informed when half her patients were incontinent? It is part of an attitude too common in nursing that, once qualified, there is no need to find out more. New innovations and changes in care pass unnoticed. The only nursing literature I saw on the ward, which was a training ward for nurses, was the copy of *Nursing Times* I brought in for them each week.

I kept my appointment to see the chief nursing officer. I arrived at the administration office to find her and her supporting nursing officers sitting round a large committee table. Their greeting was friendly and I explained what I wanted to cover in the proposed feature. One of her supporters, who knew my mother, enquired how she was.

"She is very ill," I said, explaining what had happened.

I felt this was the time to broach the subject of her care.

"Is it possible to have some better incontinence provision on the wards?" I asked.

I was not prepared for the argument which followed. I was repeatedly contradicted and told there was a wide range of provision including Kanga pants and Kylie sheets (a one-way sheet). I had already met the local Kylie sheet representative, who told me that the hospital's league of friends had bought 30 sheets for a trial and, although she said the trial results were good, there had been no further orders. I finally managed to change the subject and to get back to a friendly discussion of my feature article but why did senior managers feel it necessary to argue? Even if they had done nothing, I would have felt placated had they simply welcomed my comments and promised to look into it. In fact, they did take some action. Two weeks later the ward sister told me there was to be a meeting to discuss incontinence wear.

Meantime I bought four pairs of Kanga pants in London—none of the local chemists stocked them. I showed them to sister and the nurses on duty and put one pair on my mother. I left the rest, the instructions on the packets, in her locker. I felt elated. I had achieved something with no fuss and no bad feeling.

My elation was short-lived. Somehow the nurses could not or would not manage them. The pads were put in wrongly so that either they failed to soak up the urine or they were uncomfortable to sit on. I despaired when I found them inside out with the rubber backing next to my mother's skin. In the event, my mother very shortly solved the problem by regaining control of her bladder, but not before she had developed a bedsore which took nearly two years to disappear completely.

On top of all this, there was a string of endless irritations. My mother's eye was infected. One of her slippers was lost and never found. I had to bring in another pair. A tooth was broken off her denture—no one knew anything about it and no attempt was made to have it repaired. Her wet nighties were thrown in a heap on top of her clean ones so that they all had to be washed again—time consuming in a round of exhausting demands. At night her clothes were stuffed into her locker so that they were crumpled for dressing next day. It upset me to find her shoes wrapped in her jumper. I often felt it was a vendetta against me and my mother but I saw other patients suffer similar humiliations. The son of the patient in the next bed wept when his mother's clothes were lost and never found. The relatives of a diabetic lady complained when her insulin was frequently forgotten. Such incidents were part of life in this ward.

My mother was gradually improving. The physiotherapists asked me to bring in some of her own clothes so that she could be encouraged to try to dress herself. They suggested loose garments which buttoned down the front and trousers to make walking and exercises easier. My mother never wore trousers and so I bought her three pairs with elasticated tops.

By the middle of February—a month after her stroke—she was able to feed herself reasonably well and one person could get her in and out of bed but she still needed two people to support her while trying to walk. She was given pen and paper for the first time but she could only doodle in circles which upset her.

It was difficult to know how to occupy her. She could not read or write and the radio upset her as the language was too fast to follow. No occupational therapist seemed to be involved and it did not occur to me to seek one out. Indeed I already felt stretched to the limit of the demands I could cope with.

The book about farm animals was an immediate success

As I travel about, much of my time was spent in railway
stations with bookstalls full of large glossy picture books and I
bought her a beautiful one about farm animals. It was hard to find
clear pictures in bright colours which my mother could see with
her damaged eyes or understand with her language disabilities.
The book was an immediate success and remained a favourite to
the end of her life. The pictures of cocks, hens, pigs and horses
were taken in old-fashioned farm settings reminiscent of the farm
both of us had grown up on. Together we looked at the pictures
and I reminded her of similar animals we both remembered: a
lame duck we kept in the garden because the others attacked it
in the farmyard; Charlie the favourite white horse that my uncle
had wanted to send to the knackers (we were all so upset that
Charlie was reprieved and ended his days in the meadow behind
the house); the large and ferocious prize ram that had to be sent

back to market because no one could stop me from sneaking out to feed it. She responded to this and obviously enjoyed it as each time I arrived on the ward she pushed the book towards me. While I was away, she would study each page for ages. It was such a success that I bought her a picture book of flowers. She loved flowers but this book was not so popular.

Her enjoyment of the animal book was never marred by her inability to identify the right animal with its name. Despite this I may have been helping her to remember the meaning of words and to stimulate her understanding of language. I may also have been helping to recall her past and perhaps to fit in missing pieces. We forget there is little in a hospital ward to remind a confused or damaged brain of life outside. There are few familiar markers in the day—no shopping, no washing, no cooking and no task of responsibility to be remembered. There may be no view from the window, not even of the car park. There is no familiar next-door neighbour, milkman, dustman or paper-boy—no rain, sunshine, flowers or grass—no seasons of the year.

Staff are busy and rushed. They know nothing of the patient's real world. It is friends and relatives who bring it to the ward and jog the memory—with photographs of family, flowers from the bulbs planted last year, and news of the neighbours and the cat. A visit from a pet can be a tonic. Too often this link is neglected. Relatives struggle to fit their visits to a hospital routine and flounder, uncertain what to say when faced with loss of speech or disorientation. Embarrassed and unable to cope, they may cease to visit and the patient's best hope of recovery is replaced by drugs or psychological therapy—a poor substitute for the help a properly guided relative can give.

The Bible was another stimulus which may have helped my mother. She had been in the habit of reading her bible every night before she went to sleep. Now I read it to her. She used to follow a bible-reading course and at first I tried to continue it but it was clear that she could no longer understand it. I tried to find familiar passages which I remembered from childhood and which she seemed to recognise. On Sundays there was a service for patients in an empty office and I would take her to it. At first she would sit slumped in her chair but I soon noticed her listening attentively and nodding to the rhythm of familiar hymns. Large tears would roll down her cheeks—was it despair, frustration or a flash of recognition? Her church might have helped her and it was

41

unfortunate that both the vicar and the curate had just left and a new clergyman was starting.

My mother's household bills for electricity, gas and telephone had come in. She could not sign bank cheques and so I went to see the bank manager. My mother had struck up a good relationship with Mr Brooks, the manager of the local branch of Lloyds Bank, and with his deputy Mr Blundell. They helped her to invest her small savings providently and they were clearly very fond of her. Bank managers never feature in books on social services and where to seek help and advice in circumstances such as ours. They have a rather fearsome image—hard, like the currency of their trade.

Mr Brooks and Mr Blundell were not like that. Mr Brooks was kindly, paternalistic and filled with concern for the plight of myself and my mother. Mr Blundell too was kind as well as knowledgeable about handicaps. I came to look forward to my visits to the bank. Their staff radiated a warmth I needed and rarely felt in the so-called caring services. They had practical advice to offer on much more than money matters. When I first went to see him, Mr Brooks undertook to look after the bills and advised me to see a solicitor.

"You must get power of attorney," he said.

I had little difficulty in finding my mother's private papers. She kept them meticulously and I was thankful now that she had persisted in explaining them to me.

At the beginning of March, I saw the consultant.

"I doubt whether she will improve much more," he told me. He had prescribed prednisolone, a steroid drug, shortly before her stroke and had recently reduced the dose which was immediately followed by a rise in her ESR (erythrocyte sedimentation rate). He took this to be a poor sign and had increased the dose again. He felt she was still in danger but, if she survived, she could be in this severely handicapped state for the next five years.

"You cannot possibly manage her at home," he said. "You would be foolish to give up your job to look after her. She would not have wanted it. Her life is over. You must live yours. I can arrange for her to have a bed in the annexe."

The annexe was a long-stay geriatric unit where my mother had once been a ward sister.

My mind flashed back to Knockboy.

42

I heard my mother say, "Don't ever do this for me. Don't ruin your life," as she struggled to care for my grandmother.

I thought of home—baking bread and pastry, warm fires and cosy family meals, feeding birds, planting flowers, tea under the plum tree, drives into the country, warm sunshine and bees, children visiting, dusting, cleaning, replacing worn curtains and making beds for visitors to stay. I thought of the geriatric ward with its long lines of iron beds and high windows with no sign of birds, flowers or trees, of its daily routine of nurses washing one patient and then the next, round and round, never ending, of the ever-present smell of urine and of meals eaten at the ward table surrounded by decaying life stretching on day after day until death. Could this be home for my mother?

"Perhaps we'll look for a nursing home," I told the consultant.

"All right," he said, "but she's not ready to go anywhere yet. Come and see me in a fortnight."

My mind was in turmoil. What was I to do? The thought of my mother living on in this hopeless state was bad enough but the thought of her living in a geriatric unit or a nursing home was unbearable. I wanted to give up my job but how would we live? My mother's income was on the poverty line and mine depended on my job. Frank had financial commitments of his own— besides, we were not his responsibility. Part of me wanted her to die to be free of this hell she was living in and to relieve me of this dilemma.

"You can't give up your job," Frank said. "What would you do? Live up here? You know you'd hate it. How would I ever see you?"

"What else can I do?" I pleaded. "I won't let her go into the geriatric unit. A good nursing home might be all right if we could afford it but she can't speak."

I visualised her being left to sit for hours. I could see her bewildered, trying to make her needs known to staff too busy to comprehend. I could see her ignored by other residents who thought her mad. I could feel her pain and isolation. How would I feel, knowing this and living a life of freedom and fun?

"You have such fixed ideas," Frank said. "Lots of old people live in geriatric units and homes. What's wrong with them?" he asked. "You won't go and see anything or consider any other alternative—you can't look after her. She'll have to go in somewhere."

It was impossible to explain to Frank. He would not listen.

"O.K.," I said angrily, "I'll take you to the geriatric unit and we'll see whether you'd like to be in there yourself."

A few days later I sought out the hospital social worker. She was young, kindly and inexperienced. There were three or four solutions which seemed to suit most people's needs and she handled these efficiently. Anything other than these were beyond her. She had seen my mother on the ward and I explained our circumstances.

"I just can't let her go into the annexe," I said. "I don't like the idea of a nursing home and anyway I'm not sure we can afford it."

"Have you applied for attendance allowance?" she asked. "It's tax free and will help. She is so handicapped she will certainly be awarded the full allowance."

She handed me the forms, telling me to send them off.

"Your mother will have to be examined by a doctor from the Attendance Allowance Board and she will not be eligible until she has been severely disabled for six months but, if you apply now, it should come through as soon as she is eligible."

"Do you have a list of nursing homes?" I enquired.

She rummaged about in a drawer and produced a list of several nursing homes and rest homes.

"Can you tell me something about them?" I asked.

"Well, no," she said. "It wouldn't be ethical. We could be accused of advertising."

"You mean to say the only way I can find out how much they charge or what facilities they offer is to visit the whole lot?" I asked incredulously.

"'Fraid so," she replied cheerily.

I thought of the pile of manuscripts lying waiting to be read, of the two features I had not yet finished and of the journals and reports I still had to read to keep abreast of my work. There was my mother's tax affairs to sort out, attendance allowance to apply for and her pension to collect. There were well-meaning friends and relatives to keep informed. There was my mother to visit and feed. Her nighties needed washing, the flat needed cleaning and her house needed cleaning. There was washing, shopping and cooking to do, meals to eat and trains to catch. I had an editorial meeting in London and an interview in Manchester. Had this woman the first idea of the pressures involved? Why did none of these people offer one single practical piece of help? What a help it would have been to know details such as how much each home cost approximately, whether rooms were single or shared, and whether personal furniture and pets were allowed. Health and social service departments hold all this information and it would have helped us to short-list homes most likely to meet our needs.

"Perhaps I could find someone to look after my mother at home?" I queried.

"She's very handicapped, I don't know who you'd get," said the social worker.

"Maybe a retired nurse or an auxiliary would be interested. Perhaps I could put a notice on the hospital noticeboard?" I suggested.

"Oh no, that wouldn't be allowed," she said dismissing the idea. "We did have one family who managed to find someone to live in but it didn't work and the old woman had to come into the annexe in the end. Anyway we can't help with private arrangements. We couldn't recommend anyone—well, you do understand—if anything went wrong, we might be liable."

Frank and I agreed to spend the following weekend looking at nursing homes and I made a short list of features we thought important. In the meantime, Ann, a London friend of mine, rang me in *Nursing Times* office.

"What are you doing?" she asked. "Let me treat you to lunch."

I always enjoy seeing Ann. She is full of fun and common sense, managing to combine working as an architect with running a large house, looking after three children and entertaining the wide circle of friends she, and her husband Panos, enjoy. Over a sandwich I poured out the long saga of events.

"I really want to take my mother home but how can I find someone to look after her?" I said.

"Advertise in the local paper," said Ann. "That's what mother did for Gran and she always found someone. Mind, don't expect any arrangement to last more than a few months."

I was sceptical. I believed anyone who wanted a live-in job would want a smart house with at least a daily cleaner or even a host of helpers.

"I think you're worrying unduly," said Ann. "Gran's housekeepers did everything—there wasn't any other helper. I'm sure you'll find someone but you'll have to advertise—it's no use just hoping someone will turn up."

I went back to the office feeling better.

At my mother's house there was a letter from Aunt Emily. She wrote:

"You seem to be worried about the future and I have been awake at night thinking of it. I wonder would Adeline be happy over here? Years ago she talked of getting a house in Dublin but the prices here put an end to the idea. I suggested to Harry and Betty (my cousin and his wife) that she might come and stay with me. Of course they jumped at me—said it was too much for me. Betty said that the old dining room could be converted into a room for Adeline. I know they would be delighted to help and I would be there during the day to look after her. It's only an hour on the 'plane for you to travel. She can't stay on her own and I doubt whether she would be happy in a home. I do not know whether Betty has said this to you, but both she and Harry are full of it. Of course we must first see how she gets on . . . .''

I read the letter several times. Dear, dear Aunt Emily—she was over seventy; she could never manage my mother. She did not understand the extent of these dreadful handicaps. Betty was a qualified nurse but she was a busy farmer's wife with two children. She could not possibly take on this task. I would not expect her to.

The March weather was bright and sunny. I wanted to take my mother out to feel the spring and sunshine. It was arranged that we could take her for a drive on the first fine day. On Sunday 22 March the clocks changed to summer time and the day dawned bright and sunny. I packed a picnic. Frank and I arrived at the hospital just after lunch. We brought my mother's coat and hat and with the help of one of the nurses we got her ready for the trip. I borrowed a bedpan from the ward—just in case. The nurse found a wheelchair and helped her into the car.

We set off driving through the local streets towards her home. I pointed out familiar landmarks—her house, the local shops, the football ground and the church. There was no flicker of recognition, no response. She stared straight ahead. We drove through the country lanes to the boating lake—a favourite haunt of hers. The road alongside the lake is one way so that the lake was on my mother's paralysed right side where her vision was also restricted. Nothing could make her turn her head to look at this colourful, dancing scene of water, sunlight and sailing dinghies.

Frank searched around to find a better spot. We finally parked on a small headland overlooking the beach. There was plenty to see—parents and children playing by the water, elderly people walking their dogs, horses and riders galloping over the sand and boats bobbing on their moorings. We sat and watched a while until I produced a flask of tea and some cake. My mother drank her tea, munched her cake and stared out at the familiar scene around her. If she recognised anything or felt any emotion, it was not apparent. I felt helpless; I wanted her to enjoy this beautiful happy spring day. As we drove back to the hospital, we passed some ponies in a paddock full of waving daffodils.

I alone noticed them and I offered a small silent prayer, "God help me to survive this."

4 Coming Home

Wendy writes April–June 1981

"You can take your mother home for the weekend," the consultant told me, "but don't expect too much. I don't think she has much comprehension."

I doubted this. I noticed she had quickly worked out that the only way to hang on to her table napkin and to have it handy at mealtimes was to tuck it into the top of her pants. The physiotherapist's assistant, who helped my mother to dress each morning, told me my mother never forgot it and would refuse to sit in her chair until it was in place. I reasoned that she must have some intelligence to work this out. If so, her comprehension would improve.

Coming home even for a weekend presented a new set of problems. My mother would need a bed downstairs and a commode as there was no downstairs lavatory. We would need a wheelchair to get her from the car to the house. Fortunately my mother's house had two downstairs rooms; they had not been converted into a large through-room as in many similar houses.

Frank and I set to work to convert the dining room into a temporary bedroom. We moved the dining table into the sitting room, brought my mother's divan bed downstairs and made it up alongside the large dining room window overlooking her pretty garden. I borrowed a commode from a friend and the ward sister said we could borrow one of the many half-broken-down wheelchairs that lay about the hospital. She also agreed that we could borrow the plate surround and the cradle which kept the heavy bedclothes off her paralysed leg. I found a tomato box to serve as a backrest and we already had a bedtray for breakfast in bed. A kitchen stool became a washstand with a mirror, a plastic bowl and a towel rail beside it. These temporary arrangements would do well enough until we worked out how best to manage. Then we could borrow equipment from the council or the Red Cross.

I was nervous about taking my mother home. Would I be able to lift her, wash her and help her to dress? How would we know if she woke up in the night, wanting the lavatory? I asked staff nurse.

"Well, I don't know. I'm not on at night," she said.

"I know you're not here at night," I replied, "but haven't the night nurses recorded anything in their reports?"

"No," she said, "nothing like that."

I supposed we would find out when the time came. I hoped we would hear my mother and that she would not fall out of bed. I would have liked the opportunity to walk her, lift her and help her to dress before we left the hospital but there were no offers and I was reluctant to ask. No one enquired about our arrangements at home or suggested any equipment we might need. We were left to work it out for ourselves. I had studied the booklets on lifting and moving a stroke patient which I had bought. I hoped for the best. I was a nurse and I knew we would manage somehow but I was not surprised that so many relatives, if they took their dependant home at all, found they could not cope.

When I told my mother she was coming home for the weekend, she seemed upset. I wondered whether she did not want to come or whether she had thought she would never see home again. Perhaps she could not even remember it and did not understand what I was trying to tell her.

Frank and I took her home on Saturday morning. It took a good deal of manoeuvering to get the rickety wheelchair up the steps and through the back door into the kitchen but we finally arrived in her sitting room. She looked around in bewildered surprise and dawning recognition. Both of us started to cry. I knew she knew where she was as I pointed out familiar objects, demonstrating that nothing had been moved in her absence except the table. I explained why we had done this but I am not sure she understood.

The day went by, quietly punctuated by meals. She sat in an armchair by the fire and at mealtimes we helped her into a dining

My mother settled into her new bedroom

chair. She sat at the table and managed her food well. About 9.30 pm I helped her to bed.

"La, la, la," she exclaimed with some pleasure when she saw her bed in the dining room.

I spent a restless night going downstairs several times to see whether she was all right. In fact, she slept soundly until 8 am when I got her up to the commode. She drank a large china mug full of tea, sitting up in bed, listening to the morning service on the radio and looking out at the garden which was on her left-hand side and therefore easy for her to see. By chance we had hit on a system which I now believe helped her to recognise her paralysed right side. Every time someone came into her room she had to look to the right to see who it was.

For breakfast she ate a large bowl of porridge—a favourite of hers. She tucked her white linen table napkin under her chin, arranged it carefully with her left hand to cover her nightie and bedjacket as she hated to drop bits of food on her clothes. She ate her porridge competently. She smiled when I tipped the plate and fed her the last couple of spoonfuls.

I was worried that she might find the house cold after the heat in the hospital. There was no central heating and so I switched on an electric fire to heat up the room before getting dressed. I had carefully thought out how to wash and dress her, which paid off, as it was accomplished easily. I collected warm clothes and heated them together with a couple of bath towels in the airing cupboard. It is a good start to keeping out the cold if clothes are warm and comfortable to put on. I gathered together soap and washing things, filled the plastic bowl with warm water and set it on the stool by the bed. I positioned the wheelchair alongside the bed, covered it in a warm bath towel and explained the plan as best I could to my mother. Then I helped her to swing her legs over the side of the bed and transfer into the wheelchair while keeping her nightie out of the way so as not to sit on it.

"La, la, la," she said approvingly.

I drew the wheelchair up to the basin and mirror behind it. My mother suddenly caught sight of herself. She peered curiously at herself as though she wondered who it was. It dawned on me that she was probably seeing herself for the first time since her stroke. I had not noticed any mirrors in the hospital and it had not occurred to me to bring one in.

"You look much better now," I told her. "Your face looks fine

51

just as it always has except for your sore eye where you had the shingles but that will go in time."

She looked at me, searching my face for something. Then she lifted her limp right arm with her left hand and let it drop with a thump on her lap. Tears trickled down her cheeks.

"Cheer up," I said. "With exercise it may yet come back; besides, things could be worse. You're home for the weekend. We're getting on fine. It's a lovely day and we have a lot to be thankful for."

It was the sort of sentiment I knew she approved of.

We got on with the washing. I was careful not to do anything she seemed able to do for herself. The more independent she could be, the easier it would be to look after her. She would also be more able to fend for herself and happier. She could wash and dry her own face. I sat and watched. I helped her off with her nightie—good arm first. I washed and dried her back and good side; she washed and dried the paralysed side. Together we dressed the top half of her body, starting with the paralysed arm first. All the books about strokes explain how to do this. The theory is that, when dressing, it gives the most room for manoeuvre if the paralysed arm is the first into a sleeve. When undressing, reverse the order.

She stood up, clinging to the chair while I washed and dried between her legs. When I was finished, she sat down with a plop.

"What about the feet?" I asked. "Shall I wash your feet and legs?"

She stared at me as though working out what I had said. She started to shake her head, changing it halfway to a nod. She still got confused and was likely to shake her head when she meant to nod.

I filled the bowl with fresh water, testing it with my elbow like a baby's bath to make sure it was not too hot. I put the bowl on the floor on top of a couple of supermarket plastic bags to protect the carpet.

"Put the good foot in first so that you can feel the water. You might scald the paralysed one if the feeling's gone," I told her.

She clearly enjoyed the sensation of the warm water and kicked her foot up and down. I washed and dried the good foot and leg first and then the paralysed one.

Dressing the bottom half of her body was easy. We got pants and trousers onto the legs first; then I helped her stand up and, while she was clinging onto the chair, we hitched them up between us. When she sat down again, I put on socks and shoes. She had once made a pretty pink cotton cape which she used to drape over her shoulders while brushing her hair. I went upstairs and fetched it.

"La, la, la," she said, smiling and feeling it.

I tied the strings in a bow round her neck and gave her her hairbrush. She started to brush her hair with the back of the brush.

"The other way up," I said, turning it over for her.

She brushed her hair and combed it into place while looking into the mirror. She seldom wore make-up and grimaced with a shake of her head when I produced it.

The exercise had taken one hour. It may not have been the most orthodox method of washing and dressing but it worked. She had been thoroughly washed from top to toe without sophisticated equipment or clever expertise. What is more we had both enjoyed the rapport as I explained the plan with each step and she slowly worked it out. She followed this system of washing and dressing for the rest of her life.

We were both pleased with our efforts and laughed as I tried to coax the rickety wayward wheelchair into the kitchen. I made coffee for the three of us.

"Would you like to sit out in the sun?" I asked.

Although it was only the end of March the sun was hot in sheltered spots. Frank was washing the car; so I dressed my mother in a warm coat and hat, piled on a couple of rugs and put her to sit in a sunny spot in the shelter of the garage where she was out of the wind and could watch Frank at work. By now it was midday and I had to hurry to get the beds made, the breakfast dishes washed and the lunch prepared.

In the middle of it all, Andy rang up. Andy was my mother's best friend. Phyllis Andrews or Andy as everyone called her had come to work in the hospital when my mother was a ward sister. She was a couple of years younger than my mother and had trained as a nurse at Guy's Hospital in London. Andy had nursed in the army during the Second World War and was full of stories of hospital life in tents on battle fronts, of torpedoes and bombing at sea, of pranks with the soldiers and of her escape from Germany at the outbreak of war on the last ship to leave Hamburg for England. She had come back in the early sixties to live with her sister Dorothy while recovering from a near-fatal motor bike accident which left her disabled for a time. She wanted to get back to nursing and first came to the hospital as an unpaid volunteer. Later, as she recovered, she too became a ward sister and my mother and Andy struck up a close friendship. They shared an ethical belief in nursing, attended the same church and pursued similar interests.

"What can I do?" asked Andy on the telephone. "Shall I come and help?"

"Frank and I would love to go for a walk after lunch," I told her. "Would you come and sit with my mother to let us out?"

Andy readily agreed. I had no worries about leaving her with Andy. She was not perturbed or embarrassed by my mother's lack of speech. She chattered happily, not expecting an answer and, while she would not be able to lift my mother, she was resourceful. Andy would cheerfully tackle anything.

After lunch, Frank went to fetch Andy while I helped my mother onto the commode. Andy arrived full of bonhomie and bearing chocolates. We left the two of them settled in a pair of armchairs and already tucking into chocolates. By the time we got back, they were watching the London Marathon on television. My mother looked relaxed and happy. Sitting in her favourite chair, I almost believed nothing had ever happened.

We took her back to the hospital on Monday morning. As soon as she arrived, she seemed pathetic and miserable. She started to cry. I had tried to explain that she had to come back after the weekend because I had not managed to find help but that she would come home again next weekend. She may not have understood or she may have felt unable to face the coming week.

I felt wretched. There was no need for her to be in hospital any longer. With someone to look after her she could be in her own home where I knew she wanted to be, but looking after her was a full-time job. She could not walk or move about, wash, dress, get in and out of bed or go to the lavatory without help. She could not talk, read, or write. There was cooking, cleaning, washing and shopping to be done. Her pension had to be collected and the bills paid. I had to find someone to do this while I got on with my job in London. Somehow or other I must get her home and I must hang on to my job.

I was worried about money. It was already pouring out in fares up and down to London, in extra clothes she needed and in paying her household expenses. Her pension had been reduced to £5.45 weekly because she had been in hospital for eight weeks and without power of attorney I had no access to her savings. To assign power of attorney, the solicitor said witnesses would have to be sure my mother was aware of what she was signing. They would be unlikely to feel this at present. The court of protection which appoints a relative to administer affairs and charges handsomely for auditing the accounts was such an expensive and troublesome alternative that I wanted to wait as long as possible. I thought of appealing to the Department of Health and Social Security (DHSS) to have her pension re-instated. In the end I never did. There are only so many battles anyone can fight and this was one I was too tired and too worn out to tackle.

I judged from advertisements for housekeepers that I would have to offer at least between £50 and £70 per week plus full board and lodging (1981) for someone to live in. My mother's income was just under £50 weekly, made up mostly of income from savings she had scraped together. Her state pension was only £15.57 because of the years of unpaid insurance stamps while she had looked after her mother. (Now the DHSS pay National Insurance for anyone giving up a job to look after a dependant.) I reasoned that my mother's income would rise to £70 weekly, which would pay for a helper, if we were awarded the higher rate attendance allowance which the social worker seemed to think was certain. This was optimistic as it was not until September 1982—over one year after we started paying for full-time help—that we were finally awarded full-time attendance allowance (backdated) and then only after an exhausting battle and an appeal. Money for household expenses—gas, electricity, rates, telephone, insurance, television and household repairs—would have to be paid either by me or out of my mother's savings, which would reduce her income. There was no room for my mother to live in the flat in London and full-time daily help in London was expensive. Besides, my mother would be most likely to improve in her familiar surroundings.

I composed an advertisement: "Companion/help with nursing experience to live with elderly lady partially disabled by stroke. Comfortable home, own room, good salary. References essential." I put it under a box number in the local paper and in *The Lady*—a national magazine which carries pages of similar advertisements. I had no replies from the local paper and three from *The Lady*. I wrote to all three, explaining our circumstances and heard nothing more from any of them.

I was in despair. I now know that box numbers attract few replies. It is far better, if more inconvenient, to give a telephone number although at the time I was at work, in the hospital or travelling between London and my mother's home. It would not have been easy to give a telephone number without access to an answering machine.

I saw an advertisement for an employment agency and rang up. I spoke to a charming lady who assured me they could find me suitable help if I paid £64.40 to register on their books. I agreed to pay all fares and expenses of those they sent for interview as well as the cost of advertising. If I contracted to employ someone they sent, I was to pay the agency the equivalent of three weeks of the agreed salary. In fares and agency costs, I eventually paid out almost £500. I was shaken by the cost but I could see no alternative. The social services offer no help with private arrangements and, although jobcentres offer a free service, I found it useless. On the two occasions I used jobcentres, they failed to grasp what we needed and sent unsuitable people for interview, wasting my precious time and energy. The jobcentre regarded looking after a handicapped old lady as a sheltered, easy option for those unlikely to find jobs elsewhere. I saw it as a job requiring tact, intelligence, patience, wit and resourcefulness.

"She's gone to physio," the nurse told me when next I arrived on the ward.

"Where's that?" I enquired and she explained how to get there.

I plucked up courage and decided to ask the physiotherapists to show me how to manage. I found the department, walked in and joined my mother who was sitting doing hand exercises. The physiotherapist came over and I explained who I was.

"Nice to see you," she said. "I wish more relatives would take the trouble to come."

I nearly said, "We don't get invited." Instead I asked, "Would you show me how to help my mother?"

The physiotherapist was delighted. In five minutes I was launched into learning to lift my mother properly, splinting her knee, walking her and doing hand and arm exercises.

I was glad I had come. I had been lifting her wrongly, taking too much of her weight and doing far too much for her. Properly handled, she could move reasonably well from bed to chair or chair to chair without strain on the helper. She could manage to walk across the room with a tripod, provided that her knee was supported with a splint, but she needed an occasional steadying hand. I was so frightened of her falling that I was inclined to clutch her tight and to pull her off balance. Later I found that all helpers make the same mistake and I had to teach everyone, just as the physiotherapist taught me. Books can explain the theory but it needs a professional to show how to apply that theory to a particular patient. Poor lifting techniques are a common cause of injury to carers and pain to dependants. One patient told me it took three months for the pain in her paralysed shoulder to go after she left hospital. Each time the nurses had lifted her, they had pulled her shoulder.

Frank was worried about his boat *Iskra* which he had left laid up in America. Last year's dreams were in ashes and he would have to fetch the boat back. I was due to attend The International Council of Nursing conference in Los Angeles at the end of June and Frank wanted me to combine this with a holiday on the boat.

"How can I come?" I asked him. "I can't leave my mother and somehow or other I have to get her out of hospital."

Frank was insistent.

"You're tired and exhausted. You must get away," he urged.

To me, it seemed impossible. If I managed to get a house-keeper, I still could not go away. I had to be around to see that any arrangement was working. Besides, whoever we found would need time off. I would have to relieve at weekends. I wondered how I would manage without Frank. He listened to my jumbled emotions and half-baked plans. He mopped up the tears and jollied me along. He gave me practical help—shopping, taking washing to the laundrette, cleaning the flat, driving the car hither and thither, mending the lavatory, moving the furniture and repairing the garage roof.

Betty, cousin Harry's wife, often rang up and now she came to the rescue.

"You'll have to attend to your job," she said, "and go to the conference in Los Angeles. You'll be in America anyway and so will Frank. He's been great. He's been helping you and he deserves a bit of attention. Have a holiday with him and I'll look after Aunt Adeline."

I protested. Betty was busy, she had two children, and it was approaching the busy time on the farm. At the same time I wanted to please Frank. The prospect of a holiday held no pleasure for me—it was one more thing to be fixed and settled—something I could do without but I did want things to be all right between Frank and me. I had expected him to fade out of my life as the problems piled up. Instead he had waded in and helped. Whatever doubts I may have had about our relationship, I knew now that, if I had a future, I wanted it to be with him.

It was settled. Aunt Emily would come over before Frank left for America. Together we would take my mother to Ireland one weekend in the middle of June. I would go to the conference and have a holiday. We would also find a housekeeper to start as soon as possible.

My mother was now coming home every weekend. Each Friday evening we brought her home and I usually took her back early on Monday morning. Each weekend she made some progress. I walked her from the bedroom to the sitting room and from her chair to the table. We practised the shoulder, hand and arm exercises at the table and, when I reminded her, she would do them herself while sitting in her chair. She began to show an interest in the domestic activities and try to join in. She started to help me to make her bed. She would arrange the sheets and blankets while sitting in the wheelchair on one side while I helped on the other. She was once again the strict ward sister insisting that the bed was stripped and, to my astonishment, she tucked in perfect hospital corners with her left hand on every sheet and blanket. It took longer to make the bed but she was enjoying it and it clearly gave her a feeling of achievement. I could see her confidence grow and her dignity return as she made a contribution to these daily chores.

At mealtimes I gave her the cutlery to arrange. This demanded concentration and it would take her some time to work it out. She generally got the knives and forks the wrong way round and Frank would put them right, explaining why. It soon became a joke between them and Frank would gently tease her. Her sense of humour was returning and she would laugh happily, knowing he was poking fun. I took her out in the garden and she was soon weeding. As the beds were raised, it was easy for her to reach them.

Friends and neighbours would drop in. I was pleased they

She started to help me make her bed

came but they also presented a problem. Few of them were able to cope with my mother's loss of speech and they did not want to be left alone with her. It would have helped me if I could have left them to keep my mother company; instead I had to stay and entertain them. Although I tried to explain that my mother could understand much of what was being said, they still talked about her as if she was not there. All their remarks would be addressed to me and they would talk across her, excluding her from the conversation. This distressed me as I saw my mother shrink from it. I recalled how different it had been at Christmas. Then she had been the centre of attention and I a hovering background help. Now I was acting as a sort of embarrassed interpreter.

At worst the conversation would go: "Is your mother coming home for good?"

I would then address my mother, "Mrs A is asking whether you're coming home for good?"

"We're looking for a housekeeper; aren't we?"

My mother would nod her head, looking at Mrs A, who would then say to me, "Oh, you'll never get anything like that round here. Best let her stay in the hospital. Mrs P had a stroke and she stayed in the annexe. She died soon though—they don't last long."

I hoped my mother had missed the gist of the rapidly spoken words and I would try to change the subject.

"I hear your son has a new job?"

I found this exhausting as I tried to shield my mother from well-meaning thoughtless remarks and at the same time act as a bridge between herself and her friends. I hoped they would come to realise that my mother could understand much of what was being said and would find some way of communicating with her.

The employment agency was also starting to send prospective housekeepers for interview. They usually came from far away and Frank would have to drive some distance to meet them. I now realise that it is a mistake to employ anyone in this sort of job who does not live locally or have contacts in the district. They need to have friends and relatives to visit in their free time and it makes the job more tenable if their friends can visit them during the day.

We had decided that we needed someone with nursing experience although not necessarily a qualified nurse. Every interviewee had had some sort of previous experience in a hospital, with social services or looking after a handicapped relative. Despite this, they tended to act like some of my mother's friends and to talk across my mother, to ignore her or to treat her like a child, adopting baby talk or a 'good little dog' voice. I had no doubt that the chief barrier to finding help was my mother's lack of speech as almost everyone I interviewed could have managed her physical incapacities easily. I despaired of finding anyone.

Despite these difficulties the weekends were happy but busy and exhausting. On Monday I would get up early, help my mother to wash and dress and take her back to the hospital. She would start to cry and protest as soon as we arrived and I would feel depressed, miserable and hopeless. I discovered later that, instead of sitting facing the ward, she would insist that her chair was turned to face the wall and she sat like that throughout the week until I came to fetch her. When I left her in the hospital, I would take the car home and then catch the bus to the station—the start of my journey to London. I always carried a pile of office work to do on the train but once in my seat physical and emotional exhaustion overcame me and I often fell into a deep sleep all the way to London.

Since January I had developed an irritating pain in my left arm and shoulder until I had almost lost the power of my left arm. I dismissed it—I had no time to be ill or to bother with the rigmarole of doctors and hospitals. Besides, my mother's experience had shaken my faith in doctors and their remedies. Frank insisted I saw an osteopath and made an appointment for me in London. The osteopath was an elderly man whose rooms were simply and tastefully furnished. Everything oozed peace and tranquillity—I felt relaxed and calmed just to sit in his office. I explained the problem and his deft fingers felt my neck, shoulders and spine.

"The upper part of your spine is fixed and rigid with prolonged tension," he said. "Did you have a shock or bereavement in the last few months?" he asked.

"How do you know?" I queried.

As he massaged my aching neck and shoulder, he told me he usually found that problems with the right arm were associated with work—poor typing positions for instance. Problems with the left side were usually associated with emotional upsets. It took three consultations, combined with the regular exercises he recommended, to cure me.

Aunt Emily arrived at the end of April. Despite my warnings she was shocked to see my mother. She found it difficult to believe my mother could understand anything when she could not speak, read or write and she too tended to discuss my mother as though she was not there.

Shortly after Aunt Emily arrived, we found Mrs Richardson. She came for an interview with excellent references sent by the employment agency. She spoke to my mother, treated her as a normal person, mastered the knack of the knee splint and walked my mother well. Before leaving, she agreed to start work on the following Friday evening. I could not believe our luck as I told sister that at last we were able to take my mother home permanently. There was a flurry of activity as my mother was measured for a DHSS wheelchair of her own and the social worker arranged for a commode and bed cradle to be delivered.

I arrived back from London on Friday evening and took my mother out of the hospital for the last time. I felt a strange mixture of relief and foreboding as we said goodbye to sister at the ward door. Mrs Richardson arrived soon after we got home. She unpacked and settled into the spare room before joining us for supper. She picked at her food, rejecting this and that, but otherwise the evening passed pleasantly enough. She seemed to get on well with my mother.

We spent a disturbed night as Mrs Richardson banged about in the lavatory several times and in the morning she emerged cross and irritable. Breakfast was a disaster—she said the cornflakes tasted bad, she did not eat porridge and she only used sterilised milk and Lurpak butter. I was at a loss to know what to give her. By mid-morning the tension was rising as she announced she did not eat fish or chicken—only the best red meat. She threw all the weekend vegetables into the compost heap, declaring them rotten. My mother and Aunt Emily sat like mice. Mrs Richardson seemed to grow larger and larger, puffed up with fury as she dominated the household. I tried to calm the tension and to prepare the lunch. In the middle of the meal, Mrs Richardson stood up and announced that she was leaving. At the same time the telephone rang—Frank to say he had arrived at the station and would I please meet him.

I drove Mrs Richardson to the station. She and Frank almost collided. I started to laugh.

"Whatever's going on?" asked a puzzled Frank.

I told him the story as we drove home. I felt elated—relieved to be rid of this dreadful woman. Together with Aunt Emily we mulled over and laughed at the events of the last twenty-four hours. Aunt Emily rescued our vegetables from the compost heap, I cancelled the order for sterilised milk and my mother listened and shrugged her shoulders.

What were we to do? I had discharged my mother from the hospital. I was due back in London on Monday and at a two-day conference in Bournemouth on Tuesday and Wednesday.

"Why don't you see whether that Mrs Rigg can help?" suggested Aunt Emily.

Mrs Rigg had called to see Aunt Emily during the week while I was in London. The employment agency had sent her, mainly because she lived five minutes' walk away. She had just retired from working as a nursing auxiliary at one of the local hospitals and she had known my mother in her ward sister days. Aunt Emily had liked her but I needed someone to live in and Gladys Rigg had a husband, a dog and a house to look after. She was no use to me as she could only come during the day—but now we were in a fix. I rang her up.

"I'll come round," she said.

Gladys Rigg was short, blonde and plump. She was effusive and fussed over my mother who seemed to recognise her partially. I did not take to her much. Still, Aunt Emily would be in the house and she liked her.

"I can come in early and get your mother washed and dressed and I'll put her to bed at night," volunteered Gladys.

I explained that my Aunt could not lift my mother onto the lavatory or walk her.

"I'll come every four hours and put her on the lavatory and I'll walk her," said Gladys. "If your Aunt needs me in the night I'll come—I'm only round the corner."

I was sceptical of the arrangement and the responsibility for Aunt Emily. What if Gladys did not turn up? Would Aunt Emily be able to cope with the meals, the housework and the emotional drain my mother's plight was causing her? Perhaps I could get the social services' home help back again. I had little choice but to hope the arrangement would work. I knew the district nurses would never agree to come four-hourly or to arrive at any specified time. I had to have Gladys.

It was agreed. Gladys would come at 7 am, help my mother onto the commode and prop her up in bed. At 9.30 am she would come back and get her washed and dressed. At 1.30 and 5.30 she would help her to the commode and at 9.30 pm she would put her to bed. I would pay her £35 per week. My mother would sit in the wheelchair so that Aunt Emily could move her about. On Monday morning I showed Gladys what to do before I took the train to London. On Friday, Frank flew to America.

Aunt Emily and Gladys managed for the next six weeks; Gladys, true to her word, turned up on time, looked after my mother's personal needs, kept up the walking and exercises and above all talked to my mother with whom she developed a good relationship. She was also company for Aunt Emily who looked increasingly tired and worried. She slept badly because she was frightened of not hearing my mother at night and therefore got up several times each night to check on her.

I rang the home help organiser who had arranged for my mother's home help when she had shingles. I asked whether we could have temporary help for Aunt Emily for a few weeks. She visited while I was in London and Aunt Emily reported that help had been refused. I telephoned the organiser.

"Your aunt is managing well," she said. "Besides, if you can pay for nursing, then you can pay for domestic help. It's not as if the district nurses are visiting."

"I've been trying to get help for weeks," I explained. "It's only for a few weeks until we go to Ireland and I'm frightened my Aunt will crack up. She's over seventy and under terrific strain. You know the district nurses don't offer the sort of service we need. I have no option but to pay someone," I pleaded.

The organiser was adamant. "I can't help you," she said. "You'll have to sort it out yourself."

I felt angry and bitter. I spend much of my working time attending conferences and press briefings on health and social services. I listen to exotic claims by government ministers and bigwigs in the caring professions. I read books and reports listing pages of supposedly helpful statutory and voluntary agencies. I report government statistics—more district nurses, more home helps and more community services. My mother it seemed was too grossly handicapped to warrant a place in any of these statistics. Nobody counts those whose needs do not fit into the narrow state provision. Nobody knows how many families of old or handicapped people struggle without help. Nobody knows how many old people could or would pay for help if they knew how to find it. Nobody knows how many people are pushed into residential homes because home help organisers and managers of district nurses want them off their budget and are not prepared to help them to make private arrangements. Nobody knows how many families might carry on if a little practical help was offered at the right time.

I felt I was part of a state-supported obstacle race struggling with hospitals, social services and the DHSS.

Whichever way I turned the answer was, "No—you don't qualify; you're in the wrong place; it's not our department; we can't help."

I tore up my angry letter to the director of social services—I already knew his bland reply. I had too many other people to contact—the DHSS about attendance allowance, the appliance centre about my mother's wheelchair, the rates office about a rebate, the bank manager about the bills, the solicitor about power of attorney, the family doctor about a letter for the doctor in Ireland, the DHSS for a form for the EEC reciprocal NHS treatment in Ireland, the B & I Shipping Company about their arrangements for handicapped people on their ships to Ireland and the domestic employment agency about a housekeeper on our return. My diary was full of working appointments and deadlines to meet. The family doctor had finally secured an appointment for speech therapy and my mother had an appointment with the consultant.

Somehow or other it was all fitted in. The solicitor drew up the power of attorney document. The bank manager and the family doctor came to the house together and with Aunt Emily witnessed my mother's wobbly cross which passed as a signature. After much badgering, the DHSS delivered the wheelchair the day before we left—a week after the leaving date we had given them. I managed to see the consultant and the speech therapist.

The consultant pronounced my mother much improved, wished me luck and told me, "I doubt whether she'll live much longer."

The speech therapist said there was little she could start in the one session before our trip but in ten minutes she gave me plenty of ideas for helping my mother.

I took Friday and Monday as two days' holiday to make the journey to Ireland and to get my mother settled in over a long weekend. On Thursday evening, Aunt Emily and I packed as much as we could into my Mini, leaving room for the wheelchair, tripod and bed cradle—Betty had arranged a commode in Ireland. The Irish ferry sailed from Liverpool to Dublin at midday and we had to be on board by 11 am. It was an early start to be ready in time and Gladys came to help, promising to keep an eye on the house while we were away. My mother protested, not wanting to go. We had repeatedly explained where we were going and why, but she could not grasp it. She liked being in her own home with Aunt Emily and Gladys and it upset me to tear her away. By the time we drove up the ship's gangway I was battered and worn and Aunt Emily looked exhausted.

Nothing was too much for the ship's crew. They found the most convenient parking place near to the lift, showed us to a specially equipped cabin for the handicapped for our sole use (we had not paid for a cabin) and finally settled us on deck. It was a glorious sunny June day and, as we left Liverpool for the open sea, we began to enjoy ourselves. My mother stopped scowling and brightened up.

She began to show an interest in the other passengers and when we visited our cabin, examined the equipment curiously, exclaiming "La, la," and enjoying its convenience.

Aunt Emily and I slept in the sunshine, savouring the peace of the sea and the rhythm of the engines.

We drove through the dusk along the familiar glens and valleys of the Irish countryside. It was dark by the time we reached the last winding lane to the farm and the barking dogs heralded us into the farmyard. There were noisy greetings as helping hands unpacked us from the Mini and hustled all three of us into the large warm farmhouse kitchen. My mother gazed around in dawning recognition while Ben, the sheepdog, licked her hand and everyone else talked at once.

The weekend melted rapidly away. Betty had converted the dining room into a comfortable bedroom for my mother, the bed alongside the window overlooking the garden. I showed her my mother's routine and explained her tablets and how I coped with the bedsore. We talked about her speech and what the speech therapist and the consultant had said. Betty had had plenty of experience with stroke patients and she was full of ideas and plans.

I felt warm, safe and cossetted in the large friendly farmhouse. It was a relief to share responsibility with Betty and at last I had found someone to talk to who fully understood the implications and horror of a severe stroke. My mother knew where she was and had already acquired two constant adoring companions— Ben, the sheepdog, and Kenneth, her two-year-old great-nephew. Ben would rest his head on her lap and wag his tail as she stroked his head and talked to him.

"Lo, la, lo, la, lo," she would say—since leaving hospital her speech had acquired another vowel.

I could see what pleasure this dog gave. He seemed to understand her plight and they could be friends without the need for words.

I yearned to stay on the farm with my mother. Suppose she died while I was away? I washed and dressed her, wondering if it would be the last time. I talked to her, reminding her of times past when we had lived in Knockboy and visited this farm. I took her for a drive through the winding leafy lanes bathed in sunshine, stopping now and then in gateways to gaze over the rolling fields to the sea and the silver strand of Brittas Bay.

Two constant leisure companions

My mother's brother Willie and his wife Bessie arrived for lunch, swelling the large family party round the kitchen table. I ached with sadness as my mother sat silent, bewildered by the buzz of talk where once she would have been the centre of the conversation. I felt a strange mixture of peace, sadness and fear for the future.

On Monday evening, Betty and my mother drove me to catch the country bus to Dublin. My mother reached for my hand and held it all the way. I knew she understood that I was going away and she too feared we might never see each other again. I kissed her goodbye and the green bus bore me away to Dublin and the London aeroplane. Ahead of me stretched a week's work in Los Angeles and the three weeks' holiday with Frank, sailing up the coast of Maine.

5 Trapped

Frank writes October 1980–June 1981

I drove Wendy's Mini up to the north of England and together we collected Adeline from the hospital and took her home. She was frail, her skin like rice paper, her eyes sunk in her head, and her clothes hanging round her. Wendy stayed and looked after her until she was on her feet and then she came back to London. Life slotted back into the groove we were beginning to make for ourselves. It was not an unpleasant groove.

With anguish and heart searchings and many hesitant steps I broke with my past life, left my home, cut myself off from a whole way of living and came to stay with Wendy in the flat—for always. Now there could be no more scurrying when Adeline came to stay; my toothbrush was firmly ensconced on the bathroom shelf and I was determined it was going to stay. If a man gets his toothbrush in, I believe, he is as good as there. I spent a last Christmas with my grown-up family, sadly but without recriminations or bitterness and then I went to spend New Year with Wendy and Adeline.

Although Adeline knew quite well that Wendy and I were firmly joined together with knots more securely tied than any that could be fashioned by a priest at a wedding ceremony, she refused to accept that our union was anything but immoral and spurious. I believe she quite liked me—I did peculiar things like help to wash up the dishes, which she had never encountered in a man before and I knew how to make my bed, which astonished her greatly. We got on well. We had fierce political arguments which usually resolved themselves without blood being spilt. When I stayed in her house, she made me sleep in a separate room, which annoyed me. She moved out of her bedroom, I was installed in her bed, which I found uncomfortable, and she and Wendy slept together, in equal discomfort no doubt, in the spare room. Adeline was determined that, if there was sin in the air, which she knew there was, she would have no part of it and it would not be committed in her house. When I remonstrated with Wendy about this regime imposed by Adeline, I got no support— Wendy was clearly not prepared to wage any campaigns against her mother on my behalf. I determined that, for as long as this, to me ridiculous, hypocritical and humiliating situation persisted, I would not again come and stay in Adeline's house. My resolve was quickly overtaken by events.

I did not really know what a stroke was. Having never been ill myself, I have no more than a passing sympathy for others who are struck down. People who have strokes, I thought, either get better, except perhaps for some minor disability which persists for the rest of their lives, or they have another stroke and soon after it are dead. This, I thought, was probably what would happen to Adeline. In a strange way she seemed to have willed the stroke on herself. After Adeline had had shingles, as soon as Wendy left her in her little house, she set to work on the place with an almost neurotic fervour. She cleaned and polished and burnished it as if she were getting it ready for some great event, her own demise perhaps. She seemed convinced she was going to die.

It was typical of Adeline to make sure that, if she did die, everything would be in apple pie order.

She reiterated over and over again to Wendy her own experience with her own mother in her mind, "If anything happens to me, you're not to let it ruin your life."

As happens so often, things turned out differently from what she or any of us expected. When Wendy heard of her stroke on the telephone and together we drove north through the night in a blizzard, it was not really the beginning of an end, as I believed, but the beginning of a beginning.

As we both became involved in Adeline's illness, I began to feel trapped. It was as if she had set the snare herself and had drawn both of us into it. At first I consoled myself that she could not live for long. She was so frail when we brought her back to her house from the hospital for the second time that I thought her life would be numbered in hours, or at best days. I had reckoned without

Wendy. She did what no hospital or panel of doctors, consultants, nurses or physiotherapists could ever have done.

Wendy gave her mother another five years of life, not only life but life that had a meaning, both for Adeline and, as it turned out, for us as well. It was an astonishing display that I watched as it unfolded itself with a mixture of wonder, admiration, irritation and sometimes black despair.

She was saving Adeline's life, this frail creature whose only words were: "La, la, la, la, la, la, . . .," and at the same time she was ruining mine—at least that is how I saw it at the time.

My own life suddenly began to seem precious and brief. There was so much I wanted to do, and such a short time. Wendy had brought me a new spring—now it was suddenly endless winter with no summer in between. I had no wish to spend years looking after an old woman—an old woman I had no real reason to love.

For a time, Wendy thought she would give up her job, move north and live with Adeline until she died. I fought against this—it was a road towards poverty and dependence. With my own commitments I did not have enough money to run an establishment in the north of England, another in London where I must be to attend to my work and a third for my wife, who was in the process of divorcing me. With such a load round our necks, we would sink for certain, which would bring no good to Adeline or to any of us. I began to argue in favour of the geriatric ward of the hospital. After all, Adeline had been in charge of it herself for years—what better place for her to spend her last days in?

Wendy and I quarrelled about this—at least we came as near as we ever came to a quarrel.

In the end she said, "All right—I'll take you round there and we'll look at it."

I hate hospitals—I hate all institutions. I have a deep-seated fear of prisons; I do not know how I would live if I were ever to be sentenced to a term in prison and the hospital looked and was like a prison. We went one afternoon, in through the old workhouse door and up the stone stairs to the ward. The old ladies were in bed or sitting in chairs round one end. One, called Annie, had been in the hospital all her life. She had been born in the maternity ward 53 years ago, she had passed through several wards of the hospital during her life and now she was in the geriatric. Adeline knew her well and had grown fond of her over

71

the years she worked on the ward. Wendy herself knew her. Annie spent much of the day shouting unintelligibly.

Some sat up in bed staring ahead with vacant eyes, some had the sad, resigned look of old ladies who know there is nowhere else they will ever go, some had never been visited in months, even years, some gabbled quietly and secretly to themselves, and others greeted us like old friends, embarking on long stories about their ailments. The place smelt of disinfectant; it had a sort of dull hopelessness about it. It was clean and clinical, and the ward sister showed us round with courtesy and consideration. I knew with one glance that Wendy would never let Adeline go there to die. I was defeated.

I was beginning to worry about *Iskra* left in America; I was beginning to worry about Wendy and to worry about money. Clearly, if I had known all this was going to happen, I would never have left the boat there. It was beginning to look less and less likely that Wendy would be able to come with me when I went to fetch her. The idea of us both spending any time on board *Iskra* again seemed to become more and more remote. I could see that I would have to go to America on my own. The voyage from Providence up the eastern seaboard through Massachusetts and Maine instead of being a wonderful experience for us both would be a chore, something to be got through as soon as I could so that *Iskra* could be brought back to England as quickly as possible and laid up somewhere safe until this business was over.

The strain was beginning to tell on Wendy; she was beginning to look pale and ill, and she was jumpy and on edge. She was trying to keep down a demanding job which she did well, which she was committed to and which she cared about. *Nursing Times* were understanding and helpful towards her but only because they knew her value to them. At the same time she still was not certain about our own relationship—she had nagging doubts; half of her thought that I would cut and run when the going got tough and she did not see how she would be able to cope without help. On top of everything else was the interminable travelling backwards and forwards—the crowded trains, the journey from the station, the bus to Adeline's house, the household chores over the weekend, and the endless organising to try to get help—help from anyone, the social services, the doctor, the hospital, friends, or just people. In the end it was friends and just people who gave her what she needed.

I was worried about money because the expense of keeping this show on the road was escalating day by day. Most of the expense fell on Wendy because my own income was committed. The only way I could make any extra money was by writing another book, which is a doubtful and risky investment. Unless his (or her) work is commissioned, a writer must work hard for months with no return in the hope that he will find a buyer for his book and then that it will make him some money, both of them dubious propositions. The economics of our relationship depended on Wendy's continuing to work. If she were forced to give up, I could see nothing but ruin ahead of us.

I tried nursing homes next. Thousands of old people spend their declining years in nursing homes—they cannot all be bad. Surely it would be possible to find one where Adeline would be well looked after and reasonably happy. It was second best for her to living in her house but at least, if we could pay for it, we would be able to pursue some sort of reasonable life ourselves. I had the backing of all our friends.

To a man they chorused, "Put her in a nursing home."

Even Mrs Brereton across the road said, "You'll be putting her in a nursing home I suppose."

At that time I do not believe Adeline herself would have expressed a preference.

I could only think of her oft-repeated injunction to Wendy, "Don't you ruin your lives looking after me . . .."

On Saturday afternoons we loaded Adeline into Wendy's Mini and started off. If she was to go into a nursing home, it would have to be near her home and not in London. In London she would have no friends, and no visitors except for ourselves. In London the possibility of her ever seeing her home again would soon fade out of her mind whereas, by staying near her house, we could at least take her home at weekends. In any case, nursing homes in London were more expensive.

The nursing homes were all housed in the large, fading mansions of the once-rich local businessmen and merchants. They had gravel drives densely lined with rhododendrons, ornate porches with studded front doors, and clanging bells that rang in some inner recess when you pulled an iron handle. The old ladies and gentlemen would look at us with mild interest as we walked round. Often they sat in chairs round the walls of great halls and reception rooms, traces of former glory to be seen in decorated ceilings and fancy panelling. They were all clean and neat and tidily dressed, a few reading books or old magazines, and most staring at a point on the floor in front of them. Some watched television; some sat in their rooms looking out of the window. What they had in common was that none of them had anything to do. They were not involved in any way in the managing of or caring for their own environment. They just sat.

Old people like young people better than other old people and young people usually like old people. They feel an affinity with them. The mixing of the ages brings comfort and a sense of security and continuity. When Adeline was at home, even when she was very ill, the children from houses around the street would come and visit her. We have evolved a society that rejects old people and pushes them away out of sight behind the rhododendrons.

As we walked round, I caught Wendy looking at me and knew what was going through her mind. Adeline would be doubly isolated in any of these places. Not only would she be rendered permanently useless in every way but, having no speech, she would be quite alone and not even able to ask for her basic needs. Many of the nursing homes were managed by caring, devoted and sympathetic people. They were clean and orderly. Others were terrible places—sheets hung over the banisters to dry, the stink of urine, cruelty close beneath the surface and suffering, even fear written large on old faces. No thought of our own convenience, our own easy living, could persuade us to condemn Adeline to any of these places. I was defeated again.

When Adeline first had her stroke, we would go north every weekend, take Adeline home on Friday and back to the ward on Monday morning. We moved the furniture about so that she slept downstairs; we converted a tiny box room upstairs to a study, with a rickety card table to take the typewriter, two chairs, piles of books on the floor and an oil stove to keep us warm.

We got to know the people who lived round about—Mrs Brereton across the road, Gladys who came and helped with Adeline, and the policeman who lived on the corner. He had been a great friend of Adeline for years—never a week went past that he did not visit her; his children were always in and out of her house. From the moment she had her stroke, he never came near her again. He would see us pushing her in the street and hurry by, eyes turned the other way. Strokes and physical disabilities have strange effects on people. The policeman explained to me, apologetically, that the stroke frightened him and that he could not bring himself to have anything to do with it.

Taking her back to the hospital on Monday was traumatic, Adeline weeping in the car and Wendy in a state of acute depression. She would make the nurses turn her chair round so that she sat with her back to the ward, staring at the wall, her poor face marked down one side by scars from shingles, twisted by the stroke.

One day Wendy said, "I'm going to bring her home. I don't want her to die in that place."

It was then that Aunt Emily came from Ireland to help.

The day Adeline came out of hospital was the day she began to get better. We could see it happening week by week.

Now, when I came up on Friday she would greet me, "La, la, la, la, ..." She changed to "Do, da, do, da, do, . . ." later on.

Wendy and I began to take her for long walks round the pavements; we pushed the wheelchair at a cracking pace, which she loved. Sometimes we would load her into the Mini, and the wheelchair on top of the Mini, and take her out to tea with her friends Andy and Dorothy. Sometimes we would take the wheelchair into the country and walk with her through the lanes and along the shores of the river.

I began to understand that she was not going to die as quickly as I and everyone else had supposed. Even the consultant had told me she could not, in the nature of things, last for long. It was beginning to be evident that he was quite mistaken.

As the time came nearer for me to go to America to fetch *Iskra*, it began to look less and less likely that Wendy would come with me. Adeline demanded a huge slice of her mental and physical energy. Even when she was in the flat, half Wendy's mind was with her mother. There was never any question of us doing anything else but go to see her every weekend. If I ever had some other thing I had to do so that I could not go, I felt guilty. How would she get everything done?—washing, cleaning, shopping. One day, when I was in the flat alone, and Wendy was in the north, I found myself wondering how Adeline was—missing her. This was a shock. I thought I was proof against Adeline's subtle charms. As she got better, her personality was beginning to shine through her disabilities.

Adeline's improvement had nothing to do with hospitals or

doctors or even drugs. She was getting better because she wanted to get better. Her quality of life was way down the scale and it was clear that it could never be substantially improved. Her damaged brain would never mend however Wendy nursed her or however much love and kindness and sympathy was pumped into her.

When I went to America to fetch *Iskra*, Wendy came up with a plan to take Adeline to Ireland for a spell. She had a conference to go to in Los Angeles for *Nursing Times*. We planned that I would go to America first, spend two weeks in Providence getting *Iskra* ready for sea and then take her about one hundred and twenty miles up the Massachusetts coast to Boston in time to meet Wendy off the plane from London. We would spend a weekend in Boston together; then Wendy would go to the conference and I would take *Iskra* another hundred miles north-east to Portland, Maine. Then, the conference behind her, Wendy would have three weeks with me. She would fly back to England and I would bring *Iskra* home across the ocean. It looked too simple. I never believed for a moment that it would happen and that Wendy would really come to America.

It was Aunt Emily who first suggested that Harry and Betty might take Adeline for a month. I had never met Harry and Betty—it seemed to me incredible that they should take on this commitment and, now that I know them, I realise that it was incredible. Their life on the farm in Ireland is a cauldron of busyness—neither of them stop working from the moment they wake in the morning until bedtime. The farm is a jumble of goats and cows and chickens and bits of machinery and children and mud and confusion through which runs an inexplicable order. Keeping the whole performance together is the Irish sense of humour which everyone shares in. Adeline went to Crone and, to my astonishment, when I went to meet the aeroplane at Boston airport, Wendy came out of it.

The coast of Maine brought us as close as we had been to paradise. It is a dreamland of forests and lakes and wooded islands, vivid blue waters, the green trees all around, harbours and anchorages in abundance. Sometimes we would sail for a day in the open sea across a spacious bay, and sometimes we would thread our way through creeks and inlets, round behind islands to secret anchorages where no human sounds but our own disturbed our peace. We would wander through the shallows collecting mussels and into the woods for blueberries for supper.

76

We would swim in cool rock pools and walk through the forest to some hamlet for beer and lobster and good conversation. The mantle of worry dropped from us; we forgot about everything except ourselves. We sailed *Iskra* slowly and in peace through the glittering necklace of emerald islands and smooth reaches which is Maine. It was a kind of happiness neither of us had ever experienced before.

Maine—the closest we have been to paradise

Every few days the other present, three thousand miles to the eastward, would flash across Wendy's consciousness—we would find a telephone and talk to the girl at the International Marine Publishing Company in Camden, Maine, the publishers of one of my books.

"Nope—no message has come from Ireland," she would say, "Just you go right on having a nice time."

We took her advice so that the days tumbled over one another towards the end of our spell of paradise.

We decided to leave *Iskra* in America for another winter rather than rush through Maine and Nova Scotia. Indeed, we were incapable of hurrying—we had slowed down and moved to a lower gear; there was no urgency left in us. Surely by next year everything would have changed and we would be able to find the time we needed. I would have to take the boat into Canada and back to be allowed to leave her in the United States for another year.

All things in this life are judged by contrast—our only yardstick to beauty is ugliness; our only measure of happiness the unhappiness that has preceded it. Somewhere in Maine, I cannot remember where, I asked Wendy to marry me.

I think she must have said, "Yes."

6 Settling Down

Wendy writes July 1981–February 1982

I flew back from Boston overnight and went straight to the *Nursing Times* office from London Airport. I walked into the office feeling full of energy and plans. I tackled the pile of work on my desk with a new vigour and started to arrange visits to hospitals and health services in Ireland. This enabled me to work and help Betty with my mother until we found a housekeeper for her.

The employment agency had three possible housekeepers for me to interview, one of whom was a qualified psychiatric nurse. They felt certain that she would suit us. Betty had reported my mother to be well and Gladys Rigg said my mother's house was in good order. The only disaster was a flood in the flat. The roof had leaked while we were away and the carpet and walls were ruined. The managing agents promised to have the roof repaired and the walls redecorated. I spent the evening trying to salvage the carpet.

I flew to Dublin on Friday evening. Betty and my mother were there to meet me.

"Lo, la, lo, la, lo," said my mother, overjoyed to see me.

She looked suntanned and well and she had put on some weight. Over the weekend I noticed that she had made some progress. The speech therapist had suggested trying simple jigsaws and word-matching games. Before I left London for America, I had sent my mother a child's wooden jigsaw of a hen and chickens as well as a game called 'picture word lotto' designed to help children to recognise words by matching the word to the picture. Both were a success. My mother and Kenneth, her two-year-old great-nephew, would do the jigsaw

79

together and the 'picture word lotto' gave my mother something to occupy her while the others were busy. She also enjoyed doing it although it took three years before she could match pictures and words without a mistake. I suspect she never understood the meaning of all the words.

Giving an adult a child's game can be tricky. I did not want my mother to feel humiliated or stupid or for others to get such an impression. The children made it easier as everyone accepts it as normal for grannies to play games with children. Nevertheless, few of the games or books that belonged to Betty's children were of much use to my mother. She had difficulty distinguishing anything which was not clearly drawn and depicted in primary colours. I felt sure her colour vision was affected by either her age or the stroke.

Betty and Harry had developed an extraordinary bathing system for her. Once a week, when Harry was finished on the farm, they would help her into a kitchen chair, secure her with a sheet and carry her upstairs to the bathroom. Harry would leave Betty to help her to undress and, once she was safely covered in a bathrobe, he would come back to help to lift her into the bath. Once bathing was over, Betty would let out the water and cover my mother in towels and then Harry would come back to help to lift her out. My mother enjoyed the whole business.

She recognised its ingenuity and helped as much as she could, exclaiming "Lo, la, lo, la, lo," and chuckling with fun as she was borne aloft like a Chinese mandarin to the bath.

After the bath, Betty would cut, set and dry her hair. My mother would sit blissfully festooned in rollers while Betty or Tanya (her daughter) wielded the hair dryer. She would gaze admiringly in the mirror as Betty brushed out the curls and arranged an attractive style. Washing and bathing are an important part of many creature's relationships and its importance to humans has a long and fascinating history. Watching my mother's enjoyment, I reflected on an old people's home I had visited in Japan. They had proudly demonstrated their latest high tech equipment—a sort of old people's car wash. The old ones were put in at one end and passed along on a series of rollers, being washed and sprayed mechanically and finally spewed out clean at the other end.

"It saves nursing manpower," I was told.

Over the weekend I too washed my hair. I went out to dry it in

80

the sunshine and sat on the grass by my mother's chair. She reached for my hairbrush and started to brush my hair dry as she had done long ago when I was a child. I sat still in the sunshine as she worked confidently—left to right, brush on her lap to feel the hair, right to left, brush on her lap to feel the hair until it was dry. Strange thoughts flitted through my mind.

The consultant had said, "Her life is over; you must live yours."

Her life was not over and mine was inextricably bound up with hers. We had a way to go yet in an unexplored and treacherous territory. I had spent much of my life looking for love in all the wrong places. Now some primitive filial instinct was leading me towards it along a shadowy mine-strewn path I had not known existed.

I was surprised to hear that few relatives or friends had been to see my mother. Only Aunt Alice, her sister from Northern Ireland, and Doris, an old school-friend of mine, had been. I asked Betty why others had not come.

"They say they would prefer to remember her as she was," Betty told me.

I was angry. Was my mother to be treated like a tumble-down building or a smashed antique? What of her feelings? Was her helplessness not enough without being deprived of company and friendship? What had she done to deserve this extra punishment? I noticed that even Aunt Emily stayed in her cottage, rarely visiting the farmhouse.

Many people are unable to witness the devastation of severe handicap. It threatens, fills them with fear and lays bare their vulnerability. They suppress it, deny it and turn their backs on it, but for some it will not go away. Guilt eats and tears at the soul, causing rifts and fissures in families and friendships. Some of these relatives invited me to visit them. I did not go. If my mother was no longer fit to grace their homes, I would stay away. I would not be the sop to ease their guilt. I harboured a deep bitterness against them.

I knew that caring for my mother had not been easy for Betty. She had not had the help she expected and I suspected my mother's helplessness had roused unwanted emotions and feelings around Betty in a way she had not anticipated. I do not know. Betty is a cheerful optimist, careful to keep her own council. No trace of strain showed itself in Betty's generosity to me. There was no hint of anything but happiness as we helped my mother to blow out the candles on the birthday cake Betty had made for her. For all that, I was aware that there were strange elusive undercurrents of emotion that had not been there before. I felt guilty that Betty had been left to cope with this while I enjoyed our holiday.

I met Lucy a week later. She was the third of the three prospective housekeepers I interviewed from the employment agency. She was an attractive woman in her mid-thirties and although a qualified psychiatric nurse said she preferred to work as a nurse–housekeeper. Nurses and nursing agencies stress that nurses do not do housework. I questioned her closely on this but she assured me she would do everything—look after my mother, clean the house, cook and wash small items by hand—she would not go to the laundrette. She had worked with many stroke patients and understood their needs. I would have preferred my mother to be present at the interview as I felt it important to see how any prospective housekeeper treated her and how she reacted to them. As she was still in Ireland, I showed Lucy some photographs which she liked. She said she would be free to start work early in September and it was agreed.

I spent a week working in London and on Friday night Frank arrived from Boston—August Bank Holiday weekend. We spent it in lazy luxury in the flat. Guilt and worry evaporated in the pleasure of Frank's being home. We had spent much of our holiday discussing how to look after my mother and to keep some life of our own. We had agreed it would be simpler if we could find a house and bring my mother to live with us. On holiday on the boat in the peaceful lazy sunshine, it seemed so obvious and so easy. On Sunday we borrowed a friend's car and drove into Essex to househunt. We eventually found a large rambling old-fashioned house near Burnham-on-Crouch. It was too expensive for us and it needed endless work but in the summer sunshine it conjured up visions of garden picnics and slothful days. On the way to London I began to realise how unsuitable it was—we would have to dig ourselves out in winter and drive miles for every item of shopping. Its isolation would make it difficult to find help to look after my mother; she would see little of the outside world and, without friends to visit, the spacious rooms and garden would become a prison.

The enormity of moving at all began to dawn on me. We would

have to sell the flat and my mother's house. We would have to find a suitable house with reasonable access to our work in London. We would have to cope with chains of buyers and sellers and the inevitable breakdowns of plans. We would need time to move our belongings and to find help for my mother. We could not possibly do this while working and travelling north at weekends. Now we had found a promising housekeeper to look after my mother, we decided to leave things alone for the present.

I went back to Ireland and finished my visits for the feature articles on nursing in Ireland. Betty and Harry helped to pack my mother and me into the Mini which had stayed on the farm throughout the summer, and we set off home. It was blowing a gale and by the time we reached Liverpool it was dark and raining. Frank met us. It was a relief to relinquish the responsibility of driving. My mother was tired and I prepared a quick meal and helped her to bed while Frank unpacked the car. Next day Lucy arrived. I demonstrated the routine and arranged a list of emergency telephone numbers and an exercise book in which to record daily progress. Frank installed a baby alarm so that any movement or call from my mother at night was relayed to Lucy's bedside.

Over the next few weeks all went well. My mother and Lucy liked each other. Lucy thought of new things my mother might be able to do and I was pleased to find my mother enjoying drying up the dishes after meals—why had it not occurred to me? I noticed she was trying to move her wheelchair about with her feet and I wondered if she might be able to manage a chair she could wheel herself. The family doctor arranged appointments for speech therapy and physiotherapy at the day hospital. Lucy wheeled her there as it was only about fifteen minutes' walk. On fine days they both enjoyed the outing and, if wet, I told Lucy to take a taxi. This avoided the stress of rising early and rushing to be ready for the ambulance, waiting around until it arrived, often over an hour late, and travelling for miles, picking up other passengers on the way. It also meant that Lucy could be with my mother to talk to the therapists, to report progress and to let me know of any help we could give at home.

We had high hopes of the day hospital. Many of those who attended therapy appointments stayed to lunch, joined in various occupational activities and could also have a bath. I thought my mother would enjoy this as her bathroom was

My mother enjoyed drying the dishes after meals

upstairs and it would give her a chance to meet and observe how
other handicapped people coped. It would also give Lucy a
break. We soon abandoned the idea. Any enjoyment was marred
by the interminable pop music which dominated the day room.
While the nurses seemed to like it, the old people endured it
miserably.

There was also an unfortunate incident over bathing. The
helpers while lifting my mother managed to wrench her paralysed
shoulder. The doctor thought it was dislocated and, as there were
no X-ray facilities available in the hospital, she was sent by
ambulance to another hospital some distance away. There was
a long wait, during which time Lucy arrived having been
redirected from the day hospital. She found my mother
distressed and unable to understand what was happening or to
communicate with the staff. After the X-ray there was another
wait for the results and then for the ambulance. My mother

84

finally arrived home late in the evening, exhausted. She spent the next three days in bed with diarrhoea and vomiting which the family doctor treated. We decided that, to avoid further upheavals, my mother would only attend for the therapy sessions which were excellent. She was washed from top to toe daily and we would forego the bath.

The pattern of our weekends began to be set. We would travel from London on Friday evening and spend Saturday morning doing chores—usually heavy shopping, washing and ironing which Lucy would not do. My mother would help—washing socks, tights and small items in a basin perched on a stool, beating a cake or making the crumb mixture for pastry. She could manage these jobs with one hand, provided that they were set up for her and the bowls placed on a Dycem non-slip mat. After lunch we would take my mother for a drive. If the weather was cold or windy, we would park in a pleasant spot with a view and leave her to sit in the car for an hour while we had a walk. At first I was nervous of leaving her in case she tried to get out or to do something silly. She never did and I soon realised that she enjoyed these sessions alone. She had lived alone for much of her life and enjoyed her privacy—now she had few moments of solitude.

If the weather was nice, we would take the wheelchair and Frank would push her along the many pretty footpaths. Nowhere seemed to be too much for him. My mother would bump along happily while Frank pushed up hill and down dale over grass, rocks, stones, mud or slush—my mother loved it all. I still see her delight in one thunderstorm. Flashes of lightning lit up the sky and thunder rumbled to a loud crescendo as we rushed for shelter. The rain poured down. My mother held out her hand, catching the rain and bathing her face with it in sheer joy. I reflected that there can be few old handicapped people who have a chance to enjoy a thunderstorm.

On Sunday we would get up early for me to get my mother ready for church. Frank would retire to write in the box room which we had converted into a study. My mother had always been an active member of her church and I tried to take her every Sunday. She could follow the familiar service and see parishioners she recognised and it was an outing—a marker in the week. I also knew that her faith which she had made the basis of her life was severely shaken by her stroke.

When I read her bible to her, she would shake her head and look at me as if she was asking, "Why? Why did this happen to me?"

I tried to find her explanations as best I could, usually from her bible. Job had his faith severely tested with unbearable plagues and Jesus had had his faith tested by his crucifixion. I wished her church would help as I am not a theologian or even a regular churchgoer. They did not offer, probably because I did not ask. I felt unable to discuss it with the new vicar.

After lunch we usually visited Andy and Dorothy for tea. Andy and my mother had spent their Sunday afternoons together for many years and now her sister Dorothy invited us to tea. It followed a fixed pattern every week and we all looked forward to it and enjoyed it. After tea we would take Frank to the station from where he set off for London. My mother and I usually spent the evening looking at old photographs. I started an album and together we would sort through the piles of old photographs selecting which would go into the album. It took hours to choose

Together we would select photographs

even a few. My mother would study each one carefully, point to someone and look enquiringly at me. Sometimes it was easy and I would say who it was, reminding her with stories. Other times I gazed hopelessly at faded faces and tried to remember something about her long-dead aunts and uncles or remote cousins. She would chuckle with pleasure when she remembered. When she did not, she would place her hand over the picture and shake her head. The huge album we eventually made gave her pleasure for the rest of her life. On Monday, when Lucy arrived, I would set off for London with the pile of work I always reserved for the train.

While attending a conference in Manchester, I telephoned Frank from a call box.

"——we——married," I heard him say in the distance on a crackling line.

"What's that you say?" I shouted back.

"——," said Frank.

"I can't hear you," I yelled.

"I'm saying when can we get married?" he shouted, almost deafening me as the line came clear.

I paused. We had talked about marriage in a vague sort of way. This seemed more definite.

"Anytime you like," I heard myself say.

"I can't hear you," yelled Frank.

I shouted louder.

"I'll fix it next week," I heard him say as the line went dead.

We had to tell our relations and friends and we arranged to meet Patrick, Frank's eldest son, one evening in the pub next door to *Nursing Times* office. I was rather frightened of Frank's grown-up family. I had met Chantek, his daughter, early in our relationship and we had got on well. I had already met Patrick and after the first strained few minutes he too seemed to accept me.

As we chatted, Frank said casually, "Wendy and I are getting married."

"Great," said Patrick. "We'll have a party."

We protested—we had no time and no money. Patrick would not listen. He was determined on a party and he was already fixing it as we protested. At that time, Patrick was the skipper of a Thames sailing barge.

"You fix the date," he said, "and I'll fix the barge."

87

I wanted my mother to come to our wedding. Any mother looks forward to her daughter's wedding and I wanted her to be there.

"You can't be serious," said Frank. "Where would she stay? Who'd look after her? How would we get her on board the barge?"

I was adamant. I was not getting married if my mother could not come.

"She can stay in the flat with me and there will be plenty of strong men around. It can't be beyond their capabilities to get her into the barge saloon."

I knew he would rise to that challenge.

Before long, everyone had entered into the spirit of the wedding. My mother wept and smiled and held our hands. Her friend Andy chuckled delightedly, telling my mother how lovely it was all going to be. My mother's friends and neighbours descended on us with greetings and gifts. Ann and Panos offered us their spare room for our wedding night. Betty and Harry decided to take a week's holiday in London to attend. Frank's daughter Chantek made a wedding cake and *Nursing Times* gave us a drinks party, a large bunch of flowers and a cheque.

I felt overwhelmed by it. Somehow most of the arrangements had been taken out of our hands by kind people who wanted us to be happy. Perhaps this happens at all weddings. I had never thought about it before, having previously regarded weddings as an overrated waste of money.

The Saturday before we were married, Frank and I packed up the Mini once again and drove my mother to London. She enjoyed the drive and it did not seem to matter that despite our explanations she had no idea where we were going. When we arrived outside the flat, she recognised the building. I helped her into her wheelchair, and Frank and a bevy of passing men carried her up the steep steps into the hallway. She was delighted to see the flat.

"Lo, la, lo, la, lo," she exclaimed, gazing around.

Somehow or other we managed to squeeze my mother, her wheelchair and all her paraphernalia into the tiny two-roomed flat. She slept in the large bed with me and Frank slept on the settee. Lucy had travelled to London on the train and stayed with a friend of hers but came each day to look after my mother while Frank and I were at work.

My mother enjoyed herself—I think the flat reminded her of happy times past. I felt she was reassured that her handicap did not prevent her from sharing my bed with me. Betty and Harry and two of their friends arrived for supper and she joined in the chaotic meal I provided in the overcrowded flat. We spent the night before the wedding alone together and Frank went to stay with Ann and Panos.

I assembled our clothes for the morning and she examined each item carefully, exclaiming "Lo, la, lo, la, lo!"

She listened attentively while I explained the plan for the morning.

We were up early to have time for me to get us both dressed. I had had my mother's best coat cleaned and bought her a pair of matching trousers. Topped with a fur hat, I had bought her on a trip I made to Russia, she looked smart and examined herself approvingly in the mirror. By the time I was dressed, two of my girl-friends arrived to help us to the Chelsea Registry Office. Together we manoeuvred the wheelchair out of the block of flats, pushed it along Whitehead's Grove and through St Luke's Gardens to the Registry Office. There strong arms bore the chair aloft up the steep steps. The wedding had begun.

Looking after my mother was Lucy's full-time job. As her employer I had the same responsibilities to pay insurance and to deduct tax as any other employer. I had foolishly assumed this to be a simple matter and was horrified to receive a huge book of complicated tables from the tax office. I was expected to use these to work out exactly what should be paid. It seemed that Lucy was due £500 tax rebate which I was expected to pay her and then reclaim from the tax office. In a business, the accounts clerk pays the rebate and deducts it from the total insurance contributions the business owes the Inland Revenue. I was not a business—it had to come out of my pocket. While I was wondering what to do, a tax inspector called at my mother's house several times while I was away. He may have intended to offer help but it frightened me. I felt I could no longer cope with the continuous financial drain. Everywhere I turned, someone wanted money.

Frank found an accountant. I knew I would have to pay him too, but it seemed a protection from the terror of the tax man. It was money well spent as he found that Lucy had already registered as self-employed with a nursing agency and was working in one of the hospitals at weekends. I was absolved from further responsibility for tax rebates or PAYE. She could not be an employee and also self-employed.

One Saturday at the end of November the doctor from the Attendance Allowance Board came. He seemed a jolly little man and produced a large form. We were in the sitting room, my mother in her wheelchair by the fire. I explained to her who the doctor was and why he had come. I answered all his questions and give him the address of the employment agency which found Lucy—he wanted someone to look after his children while he took his wife on holiday. I became angry when he started to examine my mother and to comment on her disabilities disparagingly in front of her.

"She doesn't catch on very quickly, does she?" he remarked.

I felt like asking him to leave and to get out of the house. What rotten little wretch was this to come into my mother's home and assume the right to sneer at her? I said nothing. We needed the attendance allowance.

Before he left, he told me, "I think you will be awarded the day-time allowance but you are not eligible for the full allowance."

"Why ever not?" I queried. "My mother cannot be left alone at night—that's why I have to pay someone to be here all the time."

"But you don't get up several times at night to deal with incontinence," he said.

I felt like telling him that anyone who got up several times because of incontinence must not be getting the correct advice from the doctor. Instead I opened the door for him and said nothing.

A short time later we received a letter from the Attendance Allowance Board, awarding us the partial allowance. It was a blow but I accepted it. I was angry—it would have been too easy if the state really believed we needed help. It is possible to appeal and, just before the appeal time ran out, I read an article in *Nursing Times* which said that 70% of appeals are successful. I wrote away at once.

The therapy sessions were helping my mother and we noticed that her walking and movement had improved although she still needed help. She had been fitted for a full-length caliper which she could wear all day. This allowed her knee to bend when she sat down but gave it rigid support when she stood up and walked. While it was beautifully made, it was cumbersome and awkward and took time to put on. My mother never liked it and eventually it was abandoned. The community physiotherapist had visited Lucy and my mother at home and was to arrange for my mother to try a wheelchair she could manage herself. My mother's eyes had been tested at the day hospital and her existing glasses were said to be satisfactory. Despite this, I never knew her to use them again although prior to her stroke she had always used her glasses for reading.

The speech therapist's efforts too were beginning to show results. Although my mother had not regained any speech, she had improved in other ways. I was surprised to see that she had no difficulty with numbers. She could tell the time. She could put numbers in the right order and match the figures to the words—4 to four, and 2 to two. I now understood why she clearly enjoyed television quiz programmes where numbers flashed on a board, or some of the children's maths programmes. We made a point of turning them on for her. She could match some words to the pictures they described and Lucy reported that the speech therapist had said my mother's perception, listening ability and recall were good. We were given some tape recordings to use with my mother to help her to recall sounds and to try to voice them.

As my mother became more aware of her surroundings and more able to join in, she also wanted more explanations. It was not always easy to decipher what she wanted.

She would repeat, "Lo, la, lo, la, lo," endlessly and sit with her arm raised like a child in class.

At that time her face had few expressions and she had mastered few gestures to help me.

I would try whatever seemed relevant, "Do you want to go to the lavatory?" or "Is it about Lucy?"

I would go on trying until my mother would nod, smile and lower her arm. If we were getting nowhere, I would try to divert her attention but she would not give up. We then usually ended in confusion as my mother lost track of the question and I became exasperated.

Once I flounced out of the room in a fury, my head buzzing with lo, la, lo, la, lo.

I wanted to scream, to shake her and to shout, "Shut up saying lo, la, lo, la, lo."

I went upstairs and washed my hair. When I had finished, I

was calmer. I came back into the sitting room to find her distressed and sobbing. I was filled with remorse. What a horrid pig I was! I was healthy and strong with all my faculties. She was struggling in a prison far worse than bars and fences. I knelt beside her and hugged her. We sobbed together.

I was concerned that she was still on the drug prednisolone. Prolonged use can have nasty side effects such as stomach ulcers, raised blood pressure, muscle weakness, skin irritations and mental disturbances such as euphoria or depression. Her face had developed a round 'moon' appearance which I knew to be the effect of the drug. I asked Lucy to ask the consultant geriatrician at the day hospital if the drug could be reduced. It had to be reduced slowly and the consultant readily agreed, giving us a regime of reducing the drug every two weeks until my mother was off it completely.

I began to notice that Frank and I were having to do more and more chores over the weekend. Lucy would leave a list of jobs she considered were not her responsibility. The lists seemed to get longer and longer. I noticed the dust mounting under the beds and in awkward corners. The week's menu seemed to consist of more packet and instant foods, which I disapproved of. I thought my mother's clothes seemed to be changed less frequently and I was worried that she was cold as I sometimes found her inappropriately dressed in thin clothes on a cold day. It seemed that Lucy, who was fond of painting pictures and knitting, was spending more time on these activities.

Since we had agreed not to leave my mother at the day hospital and Lucy had no break, I had arranged for Gladys Rigg, who had helped before our trip to Ireland, to come on Tuesdays and Thursdays from 10 am to 3 pm to let Lucy out. I felt she needed it—five consecutive days is a long time to spend alone with an old lady unable to communicate. Gladys began to complain that Lucy was not always nice to my mother. She too disliked packet meals and had taken to bringing meat and vegetables for my mother's lunch.

Mrs Cheers, the faithful friend who had helped to feed my mother in the hospital, also came to see me. She had come to visit and found my mother trying to make Lucy understand that the television was not loud enough. Lucy had been angry, telling my mother to behave herself. She threatened to put her to bed early and finally did so, leaving Mrs Cheers distressed and embarrassed. Another neighbour told me that Lucy had asked her to sit with my mother while she went out one evening and had not returned until well after midnight.

I was upset. This was a new dilemma. Lucy had started off well and my mother had liked her. I could not bear to think that my mother was being ill-treated but it was difficult to get to the truth of the matter. It is normal for any two people living together to have a tiff or disagreement but ill-treatment is another matter. Was Lucy becoming too harassed and stressed and taking it out on my mother?

I tried to question my mother. I was not sure she understood as names seldom meant anything to her unless I could show her a photograph of the person at the same time. I had no photograph of Lucy. I got the impression from her responses to my questions that Lucy did not physically ill-treat her but no longer spent time helping her—rather ignoring her. Still I might be wrong; I could not be sure my mother understood or that I had interpreted correctly. It was only just over a week until Christmas which Frank and I would spend with my mother and Lucy would be on holiday. I decided to think about it over the holiday and, if necessary, take action in the New Year.

Before she left for her holiday, I asked Lucy whether she was finding the job stressful.

"Your mother is very difficult on Mondays and Tuesdays when you go away," she told me. "You pamper her too much and do far too much for her. I make her do more for herself and she doesn't like it."

This wounded me. I felt I was trying to encourage my mother to help herself—she was neither lazy nor apathetic. Taking her for a drive and to church could hardly be described as pampering her—they were ordinary activities she would have arranged for herself had she not been handicapped.

Lucy complained she had not had the support she had expected from neighbours. She could not get out enough and did not have enough free time. I felt this unjustified. My mother was not the neighbours' responsibility; besides, Lucy had Saturday and Sunday off each week. I also paid Gladys to relieve her on Tuesdays and Thursdays from 10 am to 3 pm and one of the neighbours sat with my mother on Monday evenings so that Lucy could attend an evening class. Wednesday was the only full day of her week. In the four months she had looked after my mother, she had had two long week-ends and was now about to have a week's paid holiday. I felt her conditions of service reasonable. I had done everything I could to make life pleasant for her.

We spent a quiet, uneventful Christmas but the Lucy problem nagged at my mind. Gladys came to visit, bearing Christmas presents—plump, generous Gladys was becoming a part of our lives. She loved my mother and the two of them enjoyed a good rapport. To Gladys the most important job any woman could do was to be a 'mum' and we were all being drawn under the spread of Gladys' motherly wings.

When my mother sulked, Gladys chivied her good-naturedly, "You tiger you, Wendy will send us both to the knacker's yard," always drew a smile.

She called Frank 'my boy' and, spotting his weakness for cake, brought him delicious offerings she had made herself.

She recognised my need for mothering and stepped into the breach by listening, advising or hustling Frank and I out of the door saying, "Off you go. Enjoy yourselves for a couple of hours and I'll look after Mrs Slack."—Gladys always called my mother Mrs Slack.

I was beginning to rely on Gladys, knowing that whatever happened she would stop up the breach until we got sorted out.

Gladys told me that Lucy had said she never stayed in any job more than six months. In any event it looked as though we would soon be searching for another housekeeper. Frank and I talked it over and our thoughts turned again to moving house.

"Perhaps we should look for something in London," I suggested.

Property at that time was still reasonably priced by London standards in Islington and around the docks. We resolved to look at these areas in the New Year.

I dreaded leaving my mother with Lucy again but, when she arrived back, my mother greeted her with coos and smiles. It must be all right, I thought, and, feeling better, left the house.

I was in *Nursing Times* office when Frank rang me. Lucy had rung him to say my mother had to go into hospital right away for a blood transfusion. The consultant was arranging an ambulance. I rang the consultant. I had not met the geriatrician to whose care my mother had been transferred.

"Yes," she said, "your mother must have a blood transfusion right away. She is very anaemic and at grave risk."

"I don't want her to go into hospital," I said. "Can't she have the transfusion at home?"

The consultant was horrified.

"I'm a trained nurse," I explained, "and so is my mother's housekeeper. We can supervise it."

"What can you be thinking of?" asked the consultant. "Call yourself a trained nurse? Don't you know the risks?"

I had once worked on the maternity flying squad for home deliveries in Liverpool and had supervised several blood transfusions in the home.

"I do know the risks," I said, "but are they greater for an old person than the risk of admission to hospital?"

There followed a sharp exchange as I detailed the time it had taken to get my mother to her present state and the speed at which I believed the hospital would reduce her to confusion, incontinence and bedsores.

I finally conceded my mother must go to hospital but I insisted that she must go by car and I must be the one to explain what was happening and take her.

"She'll be perfectly all right in the ambulance," said the consultant "and her housekeeper can come and visit her—after all she's the one who looks after her, not you."

I was furious. I saw this as typical of the arrogance and lack of understanding that so many so-called professionals exhibit.

"My mother is going nowhere until I arrive. I'll telephone you when I do," I told the consultant.

"All right," she said. "If she dies it will be your responsibility."

"I'll come with you," said Frank, but how were we to get there? There was a train strike and a snow blizzard. We queued for bus tickets with hundreds of others at Victoria coach station and finally got the last bus. There was no public transport at the other end, and so we had to queue for a taxi.

I felt frightened. If my mother died, it would be my fault—the consultant had said so. Far from being helpful, Frank made things worse.

"What are they giving her a blood transfusion for?" he asked. "She has nothing to live for. What is she being kept alive for? You must refuse to have this."

"Oh, don't be so stupid," I retorted angrily. "I've no right to

95

stop her having a blood transfusion. Only she has a right to do that."

"But she's not able to refuse—you must do it for her. She doesn't want to be kept alive," he argued.

I begged him to stop and to leave it alone. I had no reason to believe my mother did not want to live. Besides, who was I to play God? As long as there was a means of treating her, I had no right to stop it. Frank refused to listen. I wished he had not come.

Frank and I went to see the consultant early next morning. Face to face, I realised that she was probably a kind caring woman fighting battles for old people daily. She was struggling to provide a modern service in dingy, dreary buildings surrounded by inflexible attitudes and starved of money. I warmed to her. I felt sorry for her. She listened to my fears of disorientation and bedsores more sympathetically. We finally agreed on a compromise. The blood would be cross-matched for compatability at the day hospital. Once this was done, we would take my mother to the ward and she would have half the blood. We would take her home and she would come back for the second half in two days' time. We could stay with her all the time and there would be no opportunity for her to become confused or upset.

Initially the ward staff regarded us with some suspicion. Why were we having special arrangements? What was so marvellous about us? My mother was admitted to a side ward in the geriatric unit and, as it turned out, the whole business passed uneventfully. Lucy, Gladys or I sat with her in relays and she had every attention she needed. I observed that, although this ward had fewer nurses, the standard of care was much higher than on the acute medical ward where my mother had been nursed following her stroke. The reason was obvious in the two pleasant and competent ward sisters. I felt sorry that I had made such a fuss and trouble for everyone for they were kind and helpful despite the dinginess of the place. I wish now I had had enough humility to apologise.

The doctors believed my mother suffered from an auto-immune type of anaemia and had needed the blood transfusion because she had been taken off the drug prednisolone. They put her back on it. I asked whether she could try the iron tablets again which she had taken continuously for years but they dismissed the idea; I did not fully understand why. It seemed to be assumed that she no longer responded to them.

After the blood transfusion, my mother was much brighter. One Saturday evening she seemed particularly bored and tired of her few puzzles and picture books. None of us liked the choice of television programmes and I always felt awkward reading if my mother had nothing to do. I suddenly remembered playing draughts with my grandmother. Would my mother remember how to play? There was no harm in trying. I rummaged about and found the board. She watched curiously as I set the draughts out. I started with the first move, urging her to follow. To my astonishment she knew exactly how to play. What is more, she was very good at it. She laughed delightedly, enjoying the triumph as she demolished my men and kings in no time. She wanted to play again, more and more—there was no stopping her. Frank took turns to play and we all stayed up late, the three of us feeling elated.

She also remembered how to play Patience

97

The discovery of draughts was a significant milestone because it opened up a new way of communication. It was no longer necessary for friends and neighbours to be entertained by me or for them to sit awkwardly, wondering what to say. If they could play draughts, snakes and ladders or ludo or snap, which we found she could also play, the ice was broken. They could see that my mother's loss of speech did not mean she was mad or stupid and the game created a rapport that took the place of conversation. I remember that first wonderful night as a highlight in all our lives, bringing us closer together as well as creating a new freedom from each other.

At the beginning of February, Lucy told me she wanted to leave in April. I felt relieved although I dreaded the prospect of finding a replacement. As there was always someone in the house to answer the telephone, I was able to advertise in the local paper and to give a telephone number. This time the advertisement was more attractive as we had some experience of what we could offer. It read: "Housekeeper/companion with nursing experience to live with seventy-six-year-old lady Monday to Friday. Own room, comfortable home, two afternoons free, good salary, suit recently retired nurse/auxiliary, telephone ——." I also gave it to the jobcentre and typed it on postcards to put in several local shops. I asked in the health centre whether I could put it among the prams for sale and other notices on their board. They refused, probably reasonably, but it angered me. I saw it as typical of the rigid bureaucracy that stifled every initiative from relatives of the handicapped people—the very ones they should have been helping.

I wrote in my journal, "I think this health authority should have a slogan 'If it's helpful we don't do it'."

There were dozens of replies, mostly from the local paper advertisement. The telephone nearly drove us mad, interrupting, delaying and harassing us. I telephoned those that had contacted Lucy and questioned everyone closely. Most were unsuitable for reasons ranging from strained backs to not being available when we needed them. I short-listed a few and interviewed them with my mother. As usual her speech was the main problem. I watched despairingly as one after another stared at her, ignored her or treated her like a child. Finally we found Gwen, a single woman in her early thirties, who worked as an auxiliary in the geriatric unit of another local hospital. Before it was arranged, we agreed that she should come and spend an afternoon looking after my mother to see how they got on.

Meantime, relations with Lucy deteriorated. The atmosphere was strained and unpleasant. Lucy complained that my mother was impossible to manage. Gladys complained that Lucy was cross with my mother. I felt worried and harassed as well as resentful. I was now pre-cooking much of the week's food as well as coping with all the washing and ironing. I felt Lucy was acting as a weekday sitter, leaving me to do all the work at the weekend. Finally I paid Lucy a week's wages in advance and asked her to leave. It was not pleasant. She was angry and threatening and warned that we would regret pampering my mother. I did not care. I could stand the strain no longer. Somehow or other we would have to manage until Gwen was free to start.

7 Low Ebb

Wendy writes March–September 1982

Gladys stepped into the breach. She came every day from 9 am to 3 pm, looked after my mother and cleaned the house. I made arrangements to work from my mother's home as much as I could. When I had to go to London, Gladys would wheel my mother home in the afternoon and she would stay with Gladys and her husband John until it was time for bed. Together they would wheel her back to her own home and either Gladys, Glen or Christine, who lived near Gladys and worked at the hospital during the day, would stay the night. My mother liked visiting Gladys' home. She liked the coal fire and the black labrador Sam. Despite this, she often seemed depressed.

We received an appointment for my mother to attend the appliance centre to have a wheelchair test—Frank and I took the day off to take her. I was glad of his help with the driving. Unknown destinations presented difficulties if I had to unload my mother and to leave her while I found parking for the Mini. I explained where we were going and my mother co-operated expectantly in getting ready for the trip. We set off in good time and finally found the centre in an old hospital among the back streets. It was packed with people. We presented our letter and waited quietly. After a short time, our names were called and we were ushered into a large hall filled with wheelchairs. A pleasant man in a white coat asked us a number of questions and I explained that I felt my mother could manage a wheelchair she could control herself.

Manual control of a wheelchair with one hand is not easy, particularly with the left hand. The hand rims to turn the chair to the left or the right are both on one wheel and it takes intelligence to learn to use it skilfully. The therapists doubted my mother's ability but I wanted her to try. Now she refused to get out of her own wheelchair into the trial chair. Repeated explanations were useless. She had the idea we wanted to take her chair away from her and she refused to budge. I became flustered, knowing a long queue of people were waiting. The man in the white coat saved the day.

He got into the wheelchair and demonstrated.

"Now you do it," I urged. "Nobody is going to take your chair away."

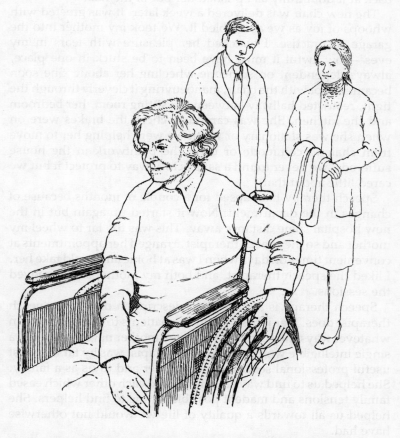

Suddenly it dawned on her that she could move herself

My mother looked doubtful but let me help her into the chair. She tried one wheelrim, then the other and then both together. Suddenly it dawned on her that she could move herself.

She set off up and down the hall at a cracking pace shouting, "La, la, la, lo, lo, lo, la, la, la," joyfully.

I was delighted and the man in the white coat smiled with pleasure.

The problem now was to stop her and to get her out of the chair. I explained that she had to be measured for the proper size and then she would have a more comfortable one of her own. She was finally persuaded to relinquish the trial chair but she looked back at it doubtfully as I pushed her out of the hall.

The new chair was delivered a week later. It was greeted with whoops of joy as we assembled it. We took my mother into the garage to practise. I watched her pleasure with tears in my eyes—how awful it must have been to be stuck in one place, always dependent on someone wheeling her about. She soon became adept with the chair, manoeuvring it cleverly through the tight, restricted hallway between the sitting room, her bedroom and the kitchen. She was careful to check the brakes were on when she was stationary or when we were helping her to move from chair to commode or bed. The paintwork in the house suffered—we never found a satisfactory way to protect it but we cared little about that.

Speech therapy had lapsed for a couple of months because of changes in the department. Now it started up again but in the new hospital some distance away. This was too far to wheel my mother and so the speech therapist arranged her appointments at convenient times on days when I was at home and could take her. I liked the speech therapist, and both my mother and I enjoyed the sessions.

Speech therapy is a misleading description of what a speech therapist does. Her job is to help her patients to communicate in whatever ways they can. Although my mother never recovered a single intelligible word, the speech therapist was by far the most useful professional service to my mother and to us as a family. She helped us to find ways to understand each other which eased family tensions and made it possible for me to find helpers. She helped us all towards a quality of life we would not otherwise have had.

I always came away from speech therapy sessions with a much

better understanding of what my mother could tackle and with new ideas to try. I realised that anything learned in childhood such as the months of the year or nursery rhymes are likely to be remembered more easily. The speech therapist helped me to become much more observant so that I could see where and when there was understanding and build on it.

For example, when the speech therapist spread common items on the table and asked, "Which is the cup?", my mother had no idea.

Yet at home when I said, "Can you set the table for tea? We need three cups and saucers," my mother had no hesitation in finding the right ones or the right number.

I noticed too that she could read the names of common foods. In the supermarket I would ask her to find a few of the items. If I asked for butter she would pick up the various packages, study the labels and select the butter. Outside a pub she would study the lunchboard. I would read out the words and she would nod at those she understood. When letters came, she would examine the name and address and we would read it, slowly pointing to each word. She also recognised some of her friends' and relatives' handwriting.

The speech therapist lent us puzzles. We bought some but they were expensive and she could not always manage them. We hit on the idea of using the local toy library and this was a huge success. The staff were helpful and soon understood what we needed. If we found my mother liked whatever we borrowed, we then bought it for her. In this way we managed to discover games and activities she enjoyed which I would never have thought of.

Without words, gestures, facial expressions and intonation of voice become much more important in communication. Immediately following her stroke, my mother's face was blank, her voice had little inflection and her gestures were few and confused. As time went on, all these improved. No one could have been in any doubt as to whether lo, la, lo, la, lo was said approvingly, disapprovingly, in horror, in amazement, to ask a question or to acquiesce. I noticed she enjoyed and learned from the television mime programmes I switched on for her. I think television in general helped to increase her range of gestures and facial expressions. These, combined with her excellent range of voice inflections, eventually meant that we seldom had any difficulty in understanding her, although in 1982 this was still in the future.

I heard there was a community craft occupational therapist employed by the social services. My mother had many beautiful pieces of embroidery and crochet work which she had made. She had also been a competent knitter and since retirement had taken up brass rubbing and pewter work, producing some attractive pieces.

I thought the craft occupational therapist might have ideas for work she could manage and would enjoy. I rang her up. She came one afternoon, laden with materials. Unfortunately she started my mother off on basketwork. My mother regarded this as a useless exercise, possibly remembering her prejudices as a ward sister—occupational therapy at that time was almost entirely equated with patients making baskets.

We bought the materials but my mother tried to avoid having anything to do with them and Gladys did most of it. I realised that it was probably a mistake. She had been such a skilled imaginative craftworker that her inability to produce work to the same standard caused her distress and frustration.

My mother was brighter since her blood transfusion but she was prone to bouts of depression she had not had before. Now, when she got some idea into her head, she persisted in trying to make us understand and she would become aggressive, cry and shout. This exhausted me as I juggled with my love for her, my failure to help her and my desire for her to stop agitating and to give us some peace. These bouts of anger were intermittent and happened with all of us—Gwen, Gladys and me. In between, life carried on as usual but the angry scenes took their toll.

I have always found relief in writing down my distress and I poured it out in my journal.

29 March, on the train to London, I wrote, ". . . . I left the house again to wails and sobs from my mother. What a relief to get away. I can't stand the endless crying and disturbance. Its persistence is exhausting and leaves me emotionally drained and frayed. Somehow or other I must get a holiday with Frank. I can't go on without a break. . . ."

4 April, on the train to London, again I wrote, ". . . .. Another dreadful weekend. My mother hardly let up for an instant and on Saturday I felt near to breaking point. I dug the front garden in the morning while my mother sat in the sun. Frank was making a

picture frame in the garage and the saw wouldn't work. He started shouting angrily, broke the saw in pieces and stamped out. At lunch-time my mother started agitating on and on and on. Frank was angry and she wouldn't shut up. I managed to hold my temper and to get washed up; then I left her alone in the sitting room and went out to the garage to Frank. I felt wretched and angry. Why are they keeping her alive on prednisolone when her life and ours are miserable? She is no longer the dignified, caring person she once was. Our days are punctuated by hourly traumas and emotional scenes. Frank went back to London on the bus on Sunday—it was a relief to have him out of the way. How am I to keep things together with Frank and to see to my mother? Gladys dropped in—my mother full of beans and laughing with her. Gwen arrived this morning and Gladys dropped in when passing. My mother turned her head away from Gwen; so Gladys started to get her up. She was shrieking and screaming when I came away. What are we to do?"

The following weekend was Easter and Gwen resigned and left on Thursday saying, "I'm sorry for you all. I don't know what you're going to do or how you'll cope."

I no longer believed this abnormal behaviour was due to my mother's stroke; otherwise why had she not reacted like this at the beginning? She did not seem to have any pain or physical ailment which might be distressing her. The more I thought about it and the more I learnt of the drug prednisolone the more convinced I was that it was causing this distress.

Easter weekend was miserable. I felt irritable and exhausted, trying to keep the peace in the house while my mother agitated and Frank looked wretched. I had to go back to London on Tuesday and once again Gladys had agreed to fill the gap while we advertised for another housekeeper. As soon as Gladys arrived, my mother started to shriek. We could do nothing with her. I called the doctor and also recorded my mother's shrieks on tape as I knew that anyone seeing her sweet smile would not believe it. As we only seemed to make her worse, Gladys and I left her and sat in the sitting room until she stopped.

The doctor was new so that I had to explain everything. He examined my mother who smiled benignly at him. I was glad I had recorded the shrieks as otherwise I am sure he would never have believed me. He gave me a prescription for a tranquilliser called Frisium, said he would telephone the consultant about reducing the prednisolone and left. I was reluctant to start my mother on a tranquilliser as they generally make old people less alert, less able to help themselves, less in control of their bodily functions and more prone to accidents. They are a slippery slope to permanent institutional care. I felt the problem was more likely to be solved by reducing the prednisolone but I doubted whether the consultant would agree to that. I started my mother on the Frisium. It made little difference and, a few days later when I struggled with another bout of screaming, I wrote bitterly in my journal: ". . . I notice that the doctor hasn't come. When she was anaemic, there was a huge fuss but, when she shrieks and screams in mental torture, no one bothers. . .."

Our advertisement attracted several replies and Mrs Aitch started immediately. She was comfortably middle aged and had spent most of her life caring for old people either in their homes or in residential care. She treated my mother nicely and they spent a happy afternoon playing draughts and ludo. My mother oozed charm and smiles and behaved perfectly while I showed Mrs Aitch how to wash and dress her and explained the routine. When I sat and watched Mrs Aitch getting her up, all went well.

Because my mother could not explain her routine or what she wanted and a new helper was not yet familiar enough to understand her efforts to communicate, I always demonstrated the routine of washing and dressing and of undressing and going to bed. I also stayed and watched until I was sure that any helper understood how to lift and move her properly and how to splint her knee and to help her to walk. The most difficult part was to persuade helpers of the importance of involving my mother in the chores. It was difficult to get them to leave the breakfast dishes until she was ready to dry them. Once a helper did understand, they often coaxed her to new achievements I would not have thought of.

I also wrote down the daily routine in some detail. Often my mother's protests were associated with failure in her routine— her hankie was not in her wheelchair, her tea was in the wrong cup or had sugar in it, or she wanted to watch a particular television programme. It helped to have a written routine to refer to. The routine was updated from time to time but this is one of the early ones.

106

8 am approximately Up to commode; dentures in; sit up in bed. Mug of tea in china mug with carnation, plenty of milk and no sugar. One tablet prednisolone.

8.30–9 am Breakfast. Large plate of porridge with a spoon of sugar and two dessertspoons bran and plenty of milk, followed by two cups of tea in white cup and saucer.

9 am–10 am Out to commode, then onto wheelchair covered in white towel and wash down; also rub bottom, clean vest weekly, clean pants daily, and different sets of clothing at least every other day. If cold, warm jumper and cardigan or blouse, pullover and cardigan. Brushes own hair and likes to help to make bed. Keeps her hankie and table napkin tucked beside her in wheelchair.

10 am–1 pm Dries up breakfast dishes. Likes to squeeze out small items of washing. Likes to help to make pastry and to watch cooking preparations. Short walk in sitting room; exercise arm by polishing the table. Likes to go to the shops in wheelchair—she carries the housekeeping purse. Puzzles or games—will do puzzles on own if set out for her. Enjoys game of draughts, snakes and ladders or snap. Cups of tea or coffee. If coffee, takes one spoon sugar.

1 pm–2 pm Lunch and lavatory.

2 pm–4 pm Sometimes short sleep in chair or on bed. Out for walk, shopping or visitors. If warm, can sit in garden or just inside garage if breezy. Put on coat and hat—keep well wrapped up.

4 pm Tea—two cups, scone or slice of cake.

5.30 pm Lavatory. Likes to help to wash up and prepare supper.

6–7 pm Supper.

8.30 pm Turn on electric blanket and fire (if cold).

9.30–10 pm Undress: commode; one tablet prednisolone, two teaspoons laxative if constipated. Dentures out; into bed. Lies on left side. Rub bottom; clothes well up and tucked round; cradle over sheet and under blanket. Likes hankie and table napkin under pillow. Turn off electric blanket; leave door ajar. Turn on baby alarm on the landing before you go to bed.

Television Likes soap operas: Coronation Street, Dallas, Emmerdale Farm, Crossroads. Family films, cooking, gardening, nature, news.

Weekly
To day hospital for speech therapy Wednesday mornings about 10.30 am.
Hoover and dust—general cleaning.
Shop for everyday items—if running low on tea and sugar, etc.
Keep a list for supermarket—I do a big store shop every so often.
Hand wash my mother's personal clothing in Stergene—nightie, vest, pants and trousers. I'll wash other woollies.
Household washing—change tea cloths, towels and one sheet and pillow case each week. Gladys will take washing to laundrette.
Ironing.

Likes and dislikes
My mother likes plain food—liver, chops, stew, roast, chicken or fish, green and root vegetables and boiled potatoes; salad; soup; beans on toast, scrambled eggs, poached egg, bacon and sausage.

Dislikes highly seasoned food such as curry. Does not like much gravy, no chips or processed food such as hamburgers or fish fingers.
Does not usually eat puddings but may have mashed banana or ice cream.

PLEASE DO NOT USE VIM ON THE BATH

Each evening when I rang from London, Mrs Aitch reported that all was well. I felt relieved—perhaps the drug was working. Perhaps my mother had been telling me she did not like Gwen. The weekend told another story. Mrs Aitch complained that Gladys was interfering. She would prefer to manage without her—she did not need time off in the week. As soon as she had gone home, Gladys arrived. She burst into tears, saying my mother had been very aggressive and had grabbed Mrs Aitch around the throat. I rang Mrs Aitch.

She dismissed it, "Oh yes," she said, "she was a bit aggressive but nothing I could not cope with."

This worried me.

"You must tell me if things like this happen," I told her.

I rang my mother's doctor. He told me to stop the Frisium. I asked again about the prednisolone.

"It's up to you," he said. "Reduce it if you want to. I'll write a prescription for Heminevrin three times daily. Can Frank come and collect it?"

Heminevrin is a sedative. Although this was prescribed in liquid form which is foul smelling and tasting, my mother did not object. The rest of the weekend passed fairly agreeably except for one screaming fit which tailed off following a dose of Heminevrin. After much heart searching, I reduced the prednisolone by half a tablet at night.

The following Friday, Gladys rang us in London. She had called the doctor and thought we ought to come as my mother seemed only semi-conscious. Mrs Aitch had called Gladys when she could not rouse my mother and it had taken the two of them to sit her up in bed. Frank and I rushed north on the train. We found my mother sleeping peacefully. The doctor had visited, could find nothing wrong and said to let her sleep. Mrs Aitch protested tearfully that she had done everything she possibly could and Gladys wept profusely. I wished they would both go away and it was a relief when they did.

I tidied my mother's room and opened the window to let fresh air into the overheated, stifling room. Then I noticed the almost empty bottle of Heminevrin—I knew what must have happened. This was the last straw—I knew I could not risk keeping Mrs Aitch. The prospect of more advertisements, more interviews, introducing yet another new person, showing her what to do and the likelihood of another failure was too much for me. I too sat down and wept.

"You can't go on like this," said Frank. "She'll have to go into hospital," he urged.

I thought of the dingy, hateful hospital. They would drug her until she stopped shrieking. All day she would sit staring into space; she would wet the bed and lose any sense of who she was or where she was. Soon she would only be alive in the sense that she was breathing. They would keep her alive with blood transfusions but there would be no drying dishes after meals, setting the table or making the bed. There would be no weeding the garden or helping to make tarts or scones. There would be nothing to give pleasure or meaning to her life.

"She's driving a wedge between us. It will tear us apart," said Frank.

I felt wretched and defeated. I knew I had failed. I must accept it. I went to the telephone and dialled my mother's doctor. He had gone off for the rest of the day. I dialled the geriatrician. She had gone away for two weeks' holiday. I felt a vague sense of relief.

"I'll try again tomorrow," I promised Frank.

In the middle of the night I woke up. A sharp stabbing pain was travelling along my left arm, my body flared hot and burning—I could not breathe. In a flash, I knew I was dying of a heart attack. Gasping, I woke Frank. He took one look, ran downstairs and dialled 999 for help. I felt myself sliding into semi-consciousness. I had not made a will—who would look after my mother? How would Frank cope?

Frank sat on the bed as I went on gasping noisily. I began to recover and to breathe more easily. A doctor arrived. Frank let him in and I heard him telling him what had happened. They came upstairs. The doctor listened to my heart and took my blood pressure. Now I was cold and shivering, my teeth chattering.

"You haven't had a heart attack," he said.

He produced three tablets.

"Take these," he said. "What are they?" I asked.

"Never mind what they are—just take them," he said.

"I don't take drugs unless I know what they are," I told him.

With some persuasion, he told me that one was Valium (a tranquilliser) and the others were pain killers. He gave me a letter for my doctor and left telling Frank that I was all right.

When he had gone, I opened the letter to my doctor.

"Anxiety state," it said.

Of course he was right—I was relieved to see it written down but why had he not told me?

From my childhood came the dear familiar long-dead Irish voice of Dr Lyons soothing me, comforting me, telling me, "Pull yourself together my girl. Sure you're fine; you're only imagining things."

Frank brought me a cup of tea and we flushed the tablets down the lavatory. Tranquillisers were no solution to my problems.

I felt groggy next day and stayed in bed except to get up briefly to dress my mother and to help her to the lavatory. Frank took charge, making the meals and looking after my mother. She was surprised and concerned to hear that I was unwell and behaved impeccably all day. I came downstairs in the evening to find Frank and my mother engrossed in a game of draughts.

Frank had to go back to London. I too should have been in London but I seemed incapable of making any temporary arrangements or of doing anything at all. I seemed to move around in a sort of unreal stillness. Gladys came during the day and I sat in the box room which we had turned into a study and did nothing. I gazed out of the window, thinking nothing and sitting immobile hour after hour. When Gladys brought coffee, I drank it. When she called me for lunch, I ate it. When she left, I sat in the sitting room while my mother had a snooze on her bed. When she got up, I switched on the television and gazed at it unseeingly. I made the supper, helped my mother to bed and went to bed myself in a kind of daze. After three days, I rang Alison at *Nursing Times* and asked for a week's holiday.

It was a sense of relief not to feel guilty about my neglected office work. I began to consider what to do next. The books say that, after a year to eighteen months, help falls away. I felt it acutely. I seldom heard from our Irish relatives and I longed for someone to relieve me of the burden of responsibility, if only for a short time. I knew that somehow I had to carry on. To do this, I was certain that I must have a proper holiday. Frank could not leave the boat in America any longer and I promised him I would have three weeks' holiday with him in Canada before he sailed back. The thought of three weeks' freedom far away from my troubles kept me going but it also seemed impossible. Somehow I had to find someone I could trust to look after my mother while I was away.

I liked Gladys' coming every day. She weathered all the storms and coped with my mother whether she was chuckling over board games or shrieking with anger. My mother liked Gladys and we all trusted her. Why not find someone willing to come from 3 pm when Gladys left and to stay the night for three or four nights weekly? Gladys was delighted with the idea and we advertised again. The rising unemployment in the north of England meant that I was swamped with replies most of which were unsuitable, but we did find Edna.

Edna was sixty and just retired from her job as a nursing auxiliary working for the community nursing services. She was small and slow and caring and, as I came to know her, I realised what a deep instinctive insight Edna had into the feelings of old people. My mother liked her and they soon became good companions. Edna seemed to cope with my mother's bouts of agitation. As the days went by, I could hardly believe that the arrangement was going to work.

At the end of May, Frank flew to America and it was agreed that I would join him in Halifax, Nova Scotia, at the end of June. I still had no arrangement for my mother but I was determined to join Frank. Gladys urged me on.

"You must spend time with your husband," she said.

I talked about it to Edna, and she and Gladys agreed that, if I could find another helper, the three of them would cope. I feared any arrangement might break down at the last moment and I reluctantly wrote to the consultant geriatrician, explaining the circumstances and asking whether my mother might have a holiday relief bed in the hospital if we were stuck. She agreed, asking that I let her know as soon as I was certain I did not need it.

I failed to find a third helper but Gladys and Edna assured me they could cope. They worked out a sensible rota between them and Gladys promised that, if it broke down, she would take my mother to her own home. I cancelled the bed in the hospital and wrote detailed instructions how to contact Frank and me through the police in an emergency. I saw the solicitor and the bank manager and gave them written instructions on what arrangements to make should Frank and I meet with disaster and fail to return. I caught up with my office work and thankfully boarded the plane to Halifax, Nova Scotia.

I came back from holiday refreshed and able to think properly again but I was apprehensive. I had left Frank in Sydney, Cape Breton, with fear in my heart. He had to sail *Iskra* back to England alone across the North Atlantic. Frank is an experienced sailor and *Iskra* a sturdy little thirty-foot boat but the North Atlantic is a cold, mean ocean and sailors disappear. As the plane soared upwards, I watched his receding sad face pressed to the airport fence and wondered what lay ahead of us. Would we see each other again?

Gladys assured me on the telephone that she and Edna could manage until I got my office work sorted out and could bring some work to my mother's home. I travelled up on Wednesday evening, taking the bus because there was a train strike. It was almost midnight by the time I arrived at my mother's house. Edna had waited up for me and welcomed me with warmth and food.

Gladys and Edna had managed but it had not been an easy three weeks. My mother seemed lethargic and subdued—she looked awful. I felt the pressure of worry closing in on me again as I saw her misery. Added to this, the rates office had written to say my mother's rate rebate had been reduced because "there were extra people living in the house". I had explained that far from contributing to the household expenses we were paying them, as my mother could not be left alone. The rates office were not impressed.

My mother had been a careful accounts keeper and I saw from her account book that since her stroke the household expenses had soared. Electricity on 6 February 1980 was £25.83; on 8 February 1982 it was £82.03. Gas on 26 February 1980 was £27.59; on 20 February 1982 it was £53.65. On an average week I was paying Gladys and Edna over £70 between them and food was costing around £30 weekly. During this time my mother's weekly

113

pension had risen by £1.31 to £16.98 and the part attendance allowance added another £15.75 which brought her weekly DHSS allowance to £32.73. Her income from savings and her NHS pension brought it to just over £60 weekly.

Had my mother been in a long-stay geriatric ward she would have been costing the state over £200 per week. We were making no demands on the district nursing or home help services. I was contributing at least £50–£70 weekly to my mother's upkeep as well as giving all my free time and energy. The only money I spent on myself was my fare to have a holiday with Frank and to pay the extra £250–£300 it cost to look after my mother while I was away. I reckoned my mother deserved her rate rebate so I wrote to the local member of parliament.

I was surprised how quickly the holiday had made me forget the mental strain of coping with my mother's agitation—the weeping and continual minor physical ailments, the headaches, eczema, tummy pain and specks of blood in her urine. These physical ailments never lasted long but they were sufficiently worrying to me to wonder whether they were the beginning of something more serious and whether I should leave her to attend to my work. I was glad to have a job because it forced me to leave the house and it forced me to concentrate on something other than the happenings in my mother's house.

I found that much of the exhaustion and worry lifted once I boarded the train for London, Manchester, Leeds or Scotland—wherever my work took me. It was an effort to turn my attentions to developments in activities such as budgeting, management or computers in nursing, but the benefits were enormous. I relished the peace and the unbroken sleep of the few nights I spent in our London flat. I looked forward to seeing office colleagues who asked about my mother and jollied me along. I was losing touch with many of my London friends and I had no doubt that without the mental stimulus and break from my mother which my job afforded me I would sink into depression and illness—I would grow to hate my mother. The love between us would have been destroyed, replaced by guilt and anger which would follow me for the rest of my life.

The summer of 1982 was hell. I worried about Frank as the days passed without any message from a passing ship. My imagination ran riot—he had been run down by a fishing boat in fog; he had capsized in a storm; he had fallen overboard or was concussed, unconscious on the cabin floor. I wondered what I would do if I heard nothing from him. I imagined the days passing without him, long after I could expect to hear from him in England. I punctuated these morbid thoughts by thinking how stupid they were. Of course Frank would turn up—he always did. I imagined the joy of his homecoming.

I was lonely without Frank. At weekends I took my mother for drives and walks but we had few visitors. Most of the faithfuls who still visited us were on holiday and, as I never knew what my mother might do if I nipped out to the local shops or even into another room, I had no time alone until the children started to visit her. Local children had always popped in to see my mother but now some new children came. We did not know their families but they came because they were on holiday with nothing to do and their mothers often seemed to be at work. They were nice children around eight or ten years old and they came to see my mother whom they liked. They saw nothing unusual about her handicaps and would happily play board games or cards with her. Sometimes they would push the furniture against the walls and put on a show for her—dances and songs they learnt at school. Often they sang nursery rhymes: 'Jack and Jill', 'Oranges and Lemons' or 'Round and Round the Mulberry Bush'. I discovered my mother remembered these as she joined in and hummed and rocked to the tunes. The children's visits also allowed me to escape into the garden or to my room for half an hour as I knew they would come for me if I was needed.

I remembered my own childhood and how I had enjoyed and sought the company of old people. These children were doing the same and, as I had, they were absorbing much about how to care for an old person. I reflected on the strange new society we live in which segregates young and old when they have so much to offer each other. I remember seeing a school in the USA where the old people of the district came and shared the children's lunch. The headmistress was astonished at the change in the children's behaviour and they had eventually been able to dispense with supervision from teachers and dinner ladies.

This led me to another reflection on local groups and societies. My mother had been an active member of the Townswomen's Guild and a helper at the church luncheon club. When she had her stroke, they sent her flowers and cards but why was she not invited back? She would have enjoyed the outing. Someone with a car might have come to fetch her. I knew these energetic ladies collected for starving Africa and protested vigorously at this and that but what about their own members? My mother had helped to serve meals at the luncheon club for years—even an invitation to the Christmas party would have been nice. Most old people are ex-employees, ex-volunteer helpers or ex-members of clubs or societies. It seems to me that if every organisation tried to take some responsibility however small for its ex-members, there would be a lot more support and relief for carers.

Meantime I had other problems as Gladys was going on holiday and Edna was being admitted to hospital for an operation on her bunion. I advertised yet again and a new stream of ladies came for interview. We took on Mrs Em to cover for Gladys's holiday and then to come at night until Edna was on her feet again.

While my mother seemed to understand what was going on and to join in some activities, she also seemed disorientated and would behave unpredictably. She would take photographs out of her album and tear them up. Once I found the floor littered with crumpled and torn pieces of cardboard puzzles the speech therapist had lent us.

On 30 July I wrote in my journal: ". . . On Wednesday Gladys helped my mother onto her bed for her afternoon nap. When she was out of the room, my mother tried to get out of bed and nearly fell on the floor. She hit her head on the side of the commode—it bled a bit. When I came back last night she was dreadful, saying "La, la, la," on and on. I think the Heminevrin is making her disorientated—says in *MIMS* (*Monthly Index of Medical Specialities*) not to give if person depressed and my mother is very depressed. We give her Heminevrin and she goes to sleep. She cries and cries when she wakes up. Mrs Cheers called and played some games with her—she brightened up. Then she got a headache—gave her two Panadol. Up at 2 am and 4 am in the night. . .."

I asked the doctor about it. He stopped the Heminevrin. He held out little hope for any improvements.

"She'll just get worse and worse until she has another stroke," he said.

Somehow I did not believe this. I felt her behaviour was linked to the prednisolone and had been aggravated by the Heminevrin.

"I'm going to reduce the prednisolone again," I told him.

"It's up to you," he said.

116

It was three months since I halved the evening tablet—now I halved the morning one.

I was worried that my mother might fall out of bed and asked the social services whether we might borrow a cot side. One morning a charming lady arrived with it. It was a horrid shiny steel thing which they use on hospital beds, incongruous and ugly in the home. My mother took one look at it and started to scream. She pushed her chair angrily towards it, grasped it and pushed it towards the door. I tried to explain. Gladys tried to explain. The charming lady looked bewildered as my mother's piercing shrieks assailed her. It was no use; she had to take it away. My mother slept on a low divan—we covered the floor with soft cushions each night in case she fell out of bed.

My appeal to the Attendance Allowance Board was now being considered and another doctor came to visit. I arranged for him to come one Friday afternoon when I was working in the north. My mother was lying on her bed when he arrived. I brought him into the sitting room—he was tall and rather aggressive to begin with, arguing that anaemia was not a disease, only a symptom. I was tired and weary, having been up three times to my mother on the previous night, and I was struggling to finish writing a feature for *Nursing Times*. I had no energy for arguing about semantics.

"Why don't you check all this with her doctor?" I said. "As far as I'm concerned, what's wrong with my mother is irrelevant. What is important is that she has to have round-the-clock care and, if I'm not here, I have to pay someone else to do it."

I answered all his questions and took him in to see my mother.

My mother looked attractive and normal lying on her bed. The tragedy of her handicap seemed the more striking as I explained who the doctor was and she smiled at him offering him her left hand saying, "La, la, la."

I warmed to him as he treated her with respect and kindness.

When I opened the door for him to go he held out his hand to me, "This is a terrible tragedy for both of you. I'm so sorry."

The kind words were genuine and unexpected. Kind words always broke down all my defences and I went back into the sitting room and wept. A short time later we were awarded the full attendance allowance and it was backdated.

Gladys rang me in London on Friday 6 August.

"Frank's safe," she said. "I've had a message from an oil rig; he'll be in Falmouth tomorrow."

117

I was filled with relief and anticipation but the message seemed peculiar and Gladys had not written down the longitude and latitude position which the oil rig radio operator had given her.

"Oil rigs are in the North Sea," I explained to Gladys. "How can he be in Falmouth tomorrow?"

Gladys did not know but she was sure that was the message. There was no doubt about it. On Sunday, Frank rang from Falmouth, safe and well. The message had come from an oil rig under tow off Cornwall.

Frank still had to sail the boat back to Essex but we spent the following weekend together in my mother's home. My pleasure in seeing him was mixed with fear of how he would react to my mother. I felt sure that, like me, he would have forgotten the strain after so long a break. I was right. Frank could not stand my mother's bouts of screaming and went to see her doctor. The doctor gave him a prescription for Bolvidon (an anti-depressant). This sent her into a deep sleep from which it was difficult to rouse her. I rang the doctor.

"Let her sleep it off," he said, "but don't give her any more. We'll try Merital instead."

This is another anti-depressant which has since been withdrawn from the market.

Although the change of drugs did not stop my mother screaming, she became more cheerful and her concentration improved. On 23 August, I wrote in my journal: ". . . The only noticeable effect of the Merital is that her concentration has improved greatly and she can spend an hour or so quietly involved in something. This means we usually have about two hours in the morning and two hours in the afternoon of respite from the wailing, raging and demanding of the rest of the day. She also smiles occasionally—something she has hardly done for three months. . .."

I found it infuriating to be given so little information about the drugs prescribed. I find it incomprehensible that patients and relatives are given almost no information about what effects a drug is likely to have. I noticed changes in my mother but, unless I searched for information in the pharmaceutical guides at *Nursing Times*, I had no idea whether these changes might be caused by the drug. Often I felt better informed than the doctor.

In Britain, doctors depend largely on *MIMS* (*Monthly Index of Medical Specialities*) for their information. This is produced by the drug industry and tends to emphasise the benefits of drugs and to minimise reactions. The DHSS Committee on Safety of Medicines is supposed to monitor drugs but they depend on the reporting of adverse reactions by doctors. Doctors are often too busy and not closely enough involved except to observe the most obvious or fatal effects. They resist any suggestion that consumers themselves are capable of reporting direct to the Committee. With no freedom of information act in Britain, consumers have no access to information from the Committee on Safety of Medicines. Even the Consumers' Association Reports are aimed at doctors rather than at the public. I found that neighbours and friends who had direct experience of prednisolone and some of the other drugs my mother was prescribed gave me far more useful information about their effects than either the doctor or the pharmaceutical guides used by doctors.

I felt certain that all our lives would be improved if we could get my mother off all drugs and onto some simple regime which would allow her to get some pleasure out of what remained of her life and would enable us to look after her and have some pleasure in our lives also. I was already reducing the prednisolone in my own way but I did not want a repeat of the blood transfusion performance. Iron had kept my mother's anaemia controlled for years and I did not understand why the doctors assumed it could not do so again. I decided to try it and bought her some iron tablets—ferrous gluconate which is a type of iron less likely to cause sickness. I also bought her vitamin C tablets; it helps iron absorption and my mother no longer liked fruit and therefore had little vitamin C in her diet.

119

8 Reconciled

Frank writes July 1981–September 1982

I have always regarded the marriage vows as a confession of mutual mistrust—how much stronger and more binding would a relationship be that survived without them, whose bonds lay deep in the heart rather than on a scrap of paper and the mumbling of a priest. It is because people cannot bring themselves to trust one another that their good faith must be circumscribed with a legal agreement. All the same, I understood clearly that I would never sell this opinion to Adeline, or to Wendy's relations in Ireland or to the good folk who lived near Adeline, or even to Wendy herself. Wendy needed a commitment and needed help and support as I did myself. Without the help, from whatever quarter it might have come, I do not believe she could have carried through what she had embarked on. I was not myself a good advertisement for the institution of marriage, having already failed at the business twice, and therefore I was surprised, when I offered the contract to Wendy, that she accepted it. Neither of us has regretted it. Marriage for us has been tremendous fun and at the same time it made our lives easier in many respects. Adeline was delighted.

I laid *Iskra* up for the winter with Tom and Toot in Sorrento, Maine. People like Tom and Toot exist in most boating communities but they are not easy to find, it usually happens by luck. Wendy and I are sometimes taken for 'yacht' people, which we are not. (There is a bit of inverted snobbery here.) We are not yachters; we are sailors, a breed common enough in England but thin on the ground in America. Yachts in America are expensive artefacts owned by rich people. They are usually painted white, often made of plastic and are adorned with expensive chrome and stainless steel fittings and expensive chrome and steel ladies in bikinis. They live in marinas where there are expensive restaurants and chandleries with all manner of costly items to tickle a rich palate. They do not often go to sea—never if the wind is above force 4.

The men wear reefer jackets and have a habit of shouting, "Say—you're on my mooring."

Iskra is old and decidedly not fashionable. We run her on a shoestring, poking about in yards and dumps for gear we can pick up cheap, doing the work on her ourselves, never visiting marinas unless forced by circumstances but preferring to lie at anchor in some quiet creek without the necessity to pay mooring fees. The first year we laid her up in America in Providence, Rhode Island, where we were lucky enough to find an excellent yard, through a friend, which was not expensive. The second year we were in despair until, by luck again, a friend told us to go and see Tom and Toot. They made their living by hauling out lobster boats for the winter in Sorrento, Maine, in just such a quiet creek as we always look for, tucked behind a green wooded island. Tom said he reckoned he could haul *Iskra* although she was bigger and heavier than the lobster boats. He made her a special cradle out of pine logs and he and Toot hauled her up the hard shore and laid her beside an old houseboat, lending me an old tarpaulin to cover her. She remained there safe and well for the freezing Maine winter. I left all my valuable gear inside her; nothing was touched. The bill at the end of the winter was $250. In fact, having *Iskra*, we spend less on our holidays than most—certainly less than we would if we went on package holidays to the continent, let alone America. The air fare to America at that time was $100—less than a first-class return train ticket from London to Edinburgh.

I met the ferry in Liverpool when Wendy brought Adeline back from Ireland and we took her to her home.

She greeted me with cries of delight, "La, la, lo, lo, la, lo, ..."—I was beginning to grow fond of this helpless old woman.

She was, of course, a different person from the fiercely independent and opinionated lady of before whose strictures had caused Wendy and me so much distress. The damage to her brain

121

had lost her a part of her character, her personality had changed, and in many respects she was not the same person.

There was no question now of, "Don't you ruin your lives for me . . .." which we had heard before.

She was clearly unaware that she had ever held such sentiments or that such sentiments even existed.

Now she was completely dependent and she looked to Wendy as the focal point of her life. She clung to Wendy like a drowning man to a stick but, at the same time, in some way she seemed to know that she could only have Wendy if she was prepared to go along with the system of life that Wendy had devised for her. Therefore, when Lucy came, she was prepared to let Wendy go to work, on the clear understanding that she would be back at the end of the week. I had the impression that she did not like Lucy much but that she would put up with her, living for the weekend when Wendy and I would be there. We went to take over every Friday evening and to give Lucy time off. We did the washing for the week—I would stagger round to the laundrette on Saturday morning, pushing a bag on a trolley. I did the odd chores and small household repairs.

For a time the arrangement seemed to work. For about four months we managed to keep it together but it ended, partly because it was ruinously expensive and partly because it soon became clear that it was impracticable. We began to see that one person alone could not be cooped up with Adeline in a small house day in and day out for a week at a stretch. This was not Adeline's fault; it was in the nature of her ailment. She was totally demanding but not through any fault of her own, and her lack of speech imposed a strain on anyone looking after her. At the same time she was still strong willed and something of a martinet.

Lucy herself became more and more demanding and less and less co-operative and helpful as time went on. I am sure this was not her fault either. The strain was formidable—the sheer uselessness of the whole operation would get under my skin and probably under hers as well. There was, inevitably, a row—Lucy was sacked, leaving Wendy with no one. Gladys stepped into the breach. It was the beginning of the system that, in the end, turned out to be the right one for us.

I did not like Gladys at first and even Wendy was undecided about her. We had been told bad things about her—wicked, destructive gossip which we did not take much notice of but which, nevertheless, left its mark for some time. In fact, Gladys was gold and we all became firm friends. One of the things we learned from the constant interviewing was that we were often wrong in our first assessment of people. Interviews, references and recommendations often left a wrong impression on us which was invariably changed by our experience of the real person. The nicest people we employed to look after Adeline had usually been the least likely candidates.

I wanted Wendy and I to be married quietly with two of Wendy's friends as witnesses. I have three children: Chantek, my daughter from my first marriage, and the two boys from my second. Wendy and Chantek got on well from the first moment— Chantek had been privy to much of my distress over the years before I met Wendy and had always given me her help and sympathy. The boys, I believe, were outraged by my decampment from the family home and my association with Wendy. They regarded her as a scarlet woman of the worst type. Her flat in Chelsea clinched the condemnation in their eyes. The young, I have noticed, are happy to embrace the permissive society for themselves but apply strict Victorian standards to the behaviour of their parents. Patrick met Wendy two or three times in London and then one evening he came to the flat for a meal. The ice between the boys and Wendy thawed slowly and with many creaks and groans but thaw it did, to be replaced with real warmth.

Patrick insisted that we should have a proper wedding and set out to organise the whole affair. He was at that time the Master of a Thames barge and he arranged for our wedding reception to be held on board. Adeline was transported to London for the occasion and installed in the flat for a few days—I slept on the settee in the sitting room but with a good grace this time, moving out to stay with Ann and Panos on the night before the wedding. Patrick turned up at the Chelsea Registry Office to be a witness resplendent in top hat and morning suit, carnation included, making a splendid entrance. I was wearing my old, comfortable sailing jacket which Wendy tore off my back as soon as she spied me.

Oonagh, the other witness, Wendy's old friend and flatmate, said, "Get out of it now, Frank—while you've still got the chance."

The Registry Office was crowded with our friends and

relations. Lunch was on board the barge, lying in the Thames outside the Prospect of Whitby. Adeline was carried on board by Harry and me up a rickety gangplank—the whole structure shuddered as it felt our combined weight, and the barge moved gently off the quay within a hair's breadth of depositing us all in the Thames. The hatches were taken off and Adeline, still in her chair, was lowered by the barge's tackle into the hold where lunch was spread.

Adeline was carried on board by Harry and me

"La, lo, la, lo, la, lo" she said, beaming round her in proud and happy contemplation of the scene.

After lunch the barge got under way and proceeded up river, the arms of Tower Bridge opened and the wedding procession berthed alongside Tower Pier. Afterwards an exhausted Adeline was taken home to the flat to bed and an evening party was held on board the barge. No one could have had a more propitious start for a marriage.

If anything, the wedding made me more anxious than ever to be off on a new tack with our lives and more impatient and frustrated by being tied, physically for every weekend and mentally because the situation with Adeline always lurked in the backs of our minds. The wedding gave us both a psychological boost but I could see that the strain was beginning to tell on Wendy. We were only just keeping even financially, both of us doing all we could to earn money only to see it dribbling away on fares and the expenses of running two households. Adeline was becoming more and more frail—she was tired and pale; she spent large tracts of the day asleep. The weekly visits north became more and more traumatic. Wendy became more and more reluctant to leave her with Lucy when the day came to go back to London; Adeline herself clearly thought she was going to die.

Against my inclination, I was becoming fond of her. She was great fun when she was in a happy mood and I could make her laugh until the tears ran down her cheeks by skylarking about and romping when she sat in the garage watching me at work on one odd job or another. She loved music—we used to listen to the classics on the radio; I would sing and shout out the words of Mozart songs just as I do when I am alone in the boat and Adeline loved it—a strong bond grew up between us. She also had fits of depression. One weekend, when she was getting very frail, she said goodbye to me when I departed for London with the clear message in her eyes and her gestures that she would never see me again—that she would be dead before another week passed. I believed her. It made me feel sad, because I had grown fond of her, but at the same time I felt that if her time had really come, it would be for the best for all of us.

It was after one of these emotional farewells, during the subsequent week, that Lucy telephoned us in London to tell us that Adeline was anaemic and that they intended to take her into hospital for a blood transfusion. We went up north at once. I was strongly against a blood transfusion and tried to persuade Wendy that it was madness. Why prolong this life? If it was my life, or Wendy's life, neither of us in the same circumstances would want it prolonged. I doubted whether Adeline, if she had been given the choice, would have opted to continue the drudgery that living had become for her. To keep people alive for the sake of it, which is what doctors seem to regard as their main mission in life, is, to me, a madness. If we have discovered how to keep people alive in defiance of nature, it is time we also discovered how to let them die if the quality of their lives and their circumstances and perhaps their own feelings all cry out for a natural demise. Wendy and I went to see the lady doctor together and I put this point of view to her.

The doctor would hardly listen. Here was a life she could save and save it she would, regardless of feelings, circumstances or ordinary commonsense. She told Wendy that, if Adeline did not have the blood transfusion, she would suffer acute pain and distress and would die in misery. I afterwards found out that this was not strictly accurate because she could have been sedated so that she felt no distress. Wendy was bowled over by her arguments and agreed to a blood transfusion. Adeline's life was thus prolonged for four years.

Life for all of us deteriorated sharply after the blood transfusion. It seemed to be the signal for what became the worst period of our lives together. Adeline was immediately stronger. She began to make life impossible for Lucy who reacted, as was natural, by treating her with less kindness. Lucy became almost as demanding of us as Adeline was, leaving a list of jobs for me to do each weekend, most of which she could have done herself. When Wendy sacked her, Gladys became our main support and helper, the most consistent and dependable helper we had among a shoal of ladies who came and went at short intervals.

Adeline was very hard to live with—my fondness for her was put to a severe test. She would shriek and shout and make such an alarming row that we thought the neighbours, indeed the whole street, would soon be complaining. When I told the doctor this tale, he prescribed different drugs, some of which made her condition worse and some better. One night I got the fright of my life.

Wendy woke up screaming and panting and unable to get her breath. I thought she was going to die and dialled 999. A doctor came quickly—a locum we had not seen before. Wendy was sitting on the bed, struggling to get her breath, her whole body pulsating and shaking, a deathly white hue, her pulse weak and her hands cold. The doctor was first rate—kind, sympathetic and firm. He calmed her down, talked to her, found out about Adeline and what was happening, took her blood pressure and pronounced that there was nothing wrong with her. He said that she was suffering from nothing more than an acute anxiety state, that such attacks often came suddenly and usually go as quickly. They are caused by stress. I suffered from a similar complaint myself, paroxysmal tachycardia, also brought on by stress. I passed through an acute attack while we were with Adeline.

After this, to me, terrifying experience I said, "Enough is enough—Adeline must go into hospital—we can't carry on with this business."

Wendy agreed but, being Wendy, with her bottomless capacity for arranging things as she wants them to be arranged, Adeline never went to the geriatric ward. There was one reason or another why the thing was delayed until, in the end, it never happened. After her attack, the doctor gave Wendy tranquillisers which she never took. She did not need tranquillisers—once she knew and understood the cause, the attack never came again.

We always took Adeline out in the car on Saturday afternoon or Sunday—it was a source of infinite pleasure to her. The tea parties with Andy and Dorothy were highlights of our visits. Dorothy would make delicious cakes; tea would be brought in on a trolley with an embroidered cloth and served from the Crown Derby.

Adeline would be all gracious and condescending; instead of saying "La, lo, la, lo," she changed to "Do, da, da, do" as time went on.

She loved the tea parties because she was included as a person in her own right and not treated as a freak or an exhibition. Andy and Dorothy were good friends to Adeline and to us as well.

We discovered wonderful walks while Adeline sat in the car, perfectly contented, for hours. After a trial of strength and persistence with the DVLC, I managed to get a free tax disc for the car—a real help. Wendy saw it, quite by chance, in a DHSS booklet she happened to pick up. She can always skiff through a document and extract anything of value to her in seconds, a talent I wish I shared. No one in the social services or the doctor told us we were entitled to free car tax for Adeline. It took a long time but eventually I tracked down the right bureaucrat at the DHSS office. After some terse correspondence he sent me the blessed form MHS330, issued, I was astonished to see, by the DHSS Scottish Home and Health Department, Welsh Office, in Dundee. I waved this multi-national document at the local vehicle registration officer and he gave me a free licence for a year. I was able to make the renewals in the normal way at a post office. The disabled person's badge, which they also gave me, was invaluable. It meant that Wendy could leave the car for a few minutes on a yellow line while she took Adeline to a shop or to the doctor. We were careful not to abuse the badge by using it when Adeline was not with us.

Joe Greene, from Sorrento, Maine, sent me a photograph of *Iskra* under Tom's tarpaulin with the snow lying thick upon her. People who have boats reserve a small corner of their minds to worry about them when they themselves are far away from the sea. After I left Sorrento, I worried about the gear I had left on board, some of it valuable and much of it irreplaceable. I had not even locked her—the place had such an ambience of simplicity and casual honesty that it had never occurred to me that anything might be stolen. The really valuable things, my sextant, chronometer, the VHF radio and the echo sounder, I had left in Tom's house, hardly more secure, I reflected, than the wooded foreshore where *Iskra* lay. The house was guarded by Tom's dog Abner, a creature whose sole desire was to lick the hand of everyone who came near. I need not have worried. Joe wrote me long letters about life in Sorrento, Maine, sent me newspaper cuttings on nautical matters he knew would interest me, inspected *Iskra* frequently and reported that all was well.

Once again, when I went out to *Iskra*, although Wendy had booked her fare, I doubted whether she would come to America. Since the blood transfusion, Adeline had been a real handful and Wendy found it difficult to get reliable people to stay, except for the faithful Gladys. It was as if Adeline was resentful and angry that she was being forced to live out this extra span of life which she did not want. She was miserable and she made everyone else miserable. I felt that, if Wendy did not get away from it for a spell she would crack—I know she felt the same. In the event she did come, leaving Adeline with Gladys and Edna whom I had not met.

I fitted *Iskra* out, waved farewell to Tom and Toot and to Joe and sailed her from Sorrento to Lunenburg in Nova Scotia, a distance of about two hundred and fifteen miles. It was a hair-raising voyage, a good shakedown for the passage home. I ran into a gale off Cape Sable, nearly put her on a reef on the eastern shore of Nova Scotia, lost myself for a spell in dense fog and passed through a large school of whales which threatened to wreck *Iskra*. I was pleased enough to reach Lunenburg, where, as usual, I found friends. Pat Fry loaned me her old motor car and I drove it the sixty-odd miles to Halifax to meet Wendy's aeroplane. I stood and watched, biting my fingernails as the plane landed and taxied to the airport terminal. The tears of relief rolled out of me as I saw her step onto the tarmac.

We had another most wonderful holiday. Everyone in Nova Scotia tumbled over themselves to be kind to us; we met new friends wherever *Iskra* went. Her red ensign was a rarity in these climes—few English yachts venture as far. I still had a number of my books on board; Wendy and I both brought out as many as we could carry from England and these paid all our expenses. Together with a few articles for magazines I wrote while we were in America and Canada the books paid all the expenses of our voyage and left some over. This was just as well as I needed money when I got back to England to shore up my much-neglected business.

Wendy and I sailed to Halifax and then through the Bras d'Or lakes in the north of Nova Scotia, a wonderful wilderness of calm waters, forests and tiny, friendly communities. We loved Nova Scotia and determined that one day we would bring *Iskra* back with more time to savour it. All too quickly our brief honeymoon passed. Unexpectedly for me, because I never had much confidence in the institution, we both got a lot out of being married. It gave our relationship some indefinable substance it never had before: it made both of us feel that we belonged, not only to one another but also to the world at large.

The airport at Sydney, Cape Breton, is a fair step from where *Iskra* lay at anchor in the bay. I walked back in a trance-like dream, not aware of where or who I was. I tumbled into the dinghy and rowed on board. Wendy was gone—suddenly taken away from me—back to Adeline, back to her worries. Somehow I had to get *Iskra* across an ocean to England—alone. Somehow, when I did get her home, I had to take up the strands of that other world ashore that I had left; it seemed an age ago. Somehow I had to make a life for me and Wendy out of this triangle with Adeline. For the moment I was frightened—Wendy had taken my courage with her in the aeroplane, leaving me weak and helpless. Two thousand miles of angry, cold, grey seas lie between Nova Scotia and Falmouth, days, weeks of solitary toil against the odds to bring *Iskra* safely across it. Had I taken on more than I could deliver?

Iskra made the crossing of the Atlantic in twenty-three days—it was a rough, wet passage but a fast one for an old lady fifty-two years old. It was the sixth single-handed crossing of the Atlantic I had made—the first in which I was lonely. I swore I would never do it again by myself—next time, if there was to be a next time, Wendy would be with me.

9 On the Move

Wendy writes October 1982–March 1984

Little by little my mother started to improve. The bouts of screaming and the minor physical complaints became less frequent. She became more alert and could concentrate for longer. She started to smile again and her keen sense of humour began to revive so that she laughed when Gladys and Frank teased her, or at the amusing trivia which is part of all our lives.

By the end of 1982 I had a reliable team of helpers. Gladys came from 9 am to 3 pm Monday to Thursday. Anna, who had replaced Mrs Em, stayed from 3 pm to 9 am on Wednesday and Thursday nights and she also stayed all day Friday until I arrived. Edna, who had recovered from her bunion operation, stayed on Tuesday night, 3 pm to 9 am and also on Monday night if I needed her. The twin beds in the spare room meant that Anna and Edna each had their own bed so that there was no need to change sheets every couple of nights.

I had worried that the constant changes of helper would upset my mother but I was wrong. Once she got to know each helper and could communicate with them, she enjoyed the change of face. My mother's activities were limited but she was not easily bored; consequently she could play several games of draughts each day. This was exhausting and irritating for one helper but quite acceptable among three. Each helper represented some change of activity or conversation as they would all tell her about the events of their daily lives.

She enjoyed this, nodding and exclaiming, "Lo, la, lo, la, lo," in surprise, approval or to query a point.

They were also pensioners near to her own age group and in time they became her friends.

131

I began to realise the advantages of a small team of part-timers. Their time with my mother was never so long that they became exasperated with her. They were all willing to cover each other for sickness or holidays so that I was able to plan my work confidently without feeling I might have to cancel plans at a moment's notice. Because they were pensioners and worked part-time, I had no worries about National Insurance contributions. It seemed so obvious and such a satisfactory arrangement in circumstances where a dependant needs familiar faces but is not easy to look after.

In September 1982 I met Diana Law at a *Nursing Times* conference in Manchester. This remarkable lady had managed to get back to living an independent life and to commanding effective speech after a severe stroke. Her book *Living after a Stroke* recounts her struggle to achieve this. She had championed the case for speech therapy and was instrumental in founding the Association for Dysphasic Adults (ADA). She also helped to set up speech clubs throughout the country. My mother's progress at speech therapy seemed to have halted and, inspired by Diana Law, I asked the speech therapist whether my mother might join a small group. I thought the competition might stimulate her and push her on a little.

At first, this seemed impossible as my mother's handicap was far more severe than most of the therapist's other patients. However, after a few weeks the speech therapist managed to find three other elderly ladies of roughly similar abilities. The little group met once a fortnight and the speech therapist went to considerable trouble to prepare special group activities for them. I watched fascinated as first one and then another would prove better than the other three. The competition did encourage them because no one person always failed and they all enjoyed it. All four of them seldom turned up as there was usually someone sick or too tired, but it did not spoil the others' enjoyment. They recognised each other and greeted each other with pleasure.

We discovered that one of the ladies lived near us. She was looked after by her husband who devoted his life to her care. He looked tired—he had had no break from his twenty-four-hour daily task which had lasted five years. I thought it might give him and his wife a break if he brought his wife to visit my mother and left her with us for a while. I asked Gladys what she thought of this idea—she was enthusiastic and so it was arranged. The first visit seemed reasonably successful but it never became a regular event. It was a good idea that did not quite come off.

The idea of moving was shelved again. Frank and I had looked at property in the east end of London. We wanted to exchange our flat for a house but any we could afford were dingy, overpriced and depressing. None of them was half as nice as my mother's little semi-detached house which would have cost four times more in London. Our flat was in a mess as the managing agents continually delayed mending the roof. Each time it rained heavily, water poured in. It would be difficult to get a good price for the flat in this state. My mother's house too was starting to deteriorate. Although she had always kept it well maintained, there was no time or money for house repairs now. I had painted the sitting room and washed much of the paintwork at weekends during the summer but the garden needed a new fence, the plumbing gave trouble and the garage needed reroofing. Much of the household equipment also needed replacing but in our present circumstances I did not want to spend the money. As unemployment rose in the north, I watched the area deteriorate and house prices fall. All around 'For Sale' signs stood unmoved month after month, year after year, and empty properties were vandalised.

I wondered how our marriage would survive another winter up and down to my mother—it troubled me. If Frank had some absorbing project, I thought we might get by. The boat had suffered from three years in America and needed refurbishing. I knew if Frank could start work on this we would pull through.

"Why don't you bring the boat north?" I suggested.

Frank liked the idea and started to investigate the possibility. It seemed too complicated and in the end we compromised. Everything that could be removed from *Iskra*—shelves, locker doors, table, spars and rigging—was brought up and Frank spent his weekends in the garage stripping paint and revarnishing.

There was still time to take my mother for drives and outings, to tea with Andy and Dorothy and sometimes to the shops. Occasionally we went further afield for picnics in the hills. We all enjoyed these drives and my mother would sleep in the car while Frank and I went for walks. As there were no accessible lavatories I would take a bedpan for my mother. Frank would park in a secluded place, I would open the car door, hang a rug over the window, place the wheelchair alongside the car, remove its

133

cushions and put the bedpan on the seat protected by a couple of sheets of kitchen paper. Portable commodes are expensive and not easy to hire, but this arrangement worked well and took up little space in our Mini.

Occasionally we went further afield for picnics in the hills

As Christmas 1982 approached, Gladys and my mother made several forays to the shops to choose presents for Frank and me and for other friends and neighbours. Together they wrapped them up and Gladys wrote a greeting on a piece of paper which my mother laboriously copied onto each card.

We spent a happy Christmas with my mother at her home and enjoyed a brief visit from Betty and Harry in the New Year. I asked my mother's doctor whether he would like to come and see her. Over six months I had halved the prednisolone from ten milligrams daily to five milligrams, and I could no longer reduce it without a prescription for a smaller dose. The doctor was pleased with her. She looked well with no sign of anaemia and the bouts of screaming were much less frequent and more tolerable. He suggested that we reduce the prednisolone by one milligram each fortnight. She took the last dose on 13 March but I kept giving her the iron tablets and vitamin C. She was still taking the tranquilliser Merital and the doctor thought it advisable to wait a while before reducing it.

The question of restoring the rate rebate was still being pursued and I received a letter from our member of parliament to say that the council had relented and restored it in full. He had also raised the matter with the appropriate minister so that the rules were changed to make it clear that no deduction should be made in circumstances such as my mother's. I wrote to thank him and a few days later we received the rebate in full.

In March 1983, Alison told me she was leaving her job as editor of *Nursing Times*. This was a worry. A new editor would have new ideas on how to run the journal and to use the staff. I was spending half my working week in the north of England; a new editor might not see the need for this. Alison had always been sympathetic to my circumstances and I believed this was because she was a woman, with a family and children of her own. I thought a man would see things differently.

Alison's impending departure caused unrest and uncertainty throughout the office. *Nursing Times* had always been a happy place to work; now factions and fissures began to appear as gossip and rumour multiplied about who might get the editor's job.

As Alison's departure approached, one of my mother's helpers, Anna, developed problems of her own and decided first to cut down her hours and then to leave so that I was faced with a new round of advertising. This always upset me, as interviewing, selecting and introducing a new person exhausted me and disturbed my mother. Among other upsets, she usually went through a routine of making Gladys or me open all the cupboards and drawers while she inspected in case anything had been stolen. Any misplaced item had to be accounted for and this often led to endless upheavals and searchings—I once spent a whole Saturday unpacking cases from the loft to find a salt cellar. In fact, nothing was ever stolen. After two or three weeks, things usually settled down or the helper left and we started all over again.

I felt tired and longed for some time to myself. My life was devoted to my mother, to Frank, to housekeeping and to my work. I needed new underwear and I had not bought a new item of clothing in three years—there was no time for me to browse alone in the shops. My hair had grown long because I had no time or money for hairdressers—I bundled it up with pins and clips and left it to its own devices. I avoided looking in the mirror. In 1980 I was a self-confident young and lively woman; now, three years later, my confidence had ebbed and I was grey and middle aged. I noticed my memory had deteriorated; I forgot things quickly and had to be careful to write down any arrangements or plans, particularly in my job. I picked up a photograph of my mother at my age when she was looking after Granny in Knockboy. It showed the knuckles of her clenched hands, her face strained and her hair pinned up in the same untidy way. I saw myself in her.

I had one trump card and we decided it was nearly time to play it. I was due three months' sabbatical leave from my work, and Frank and I decided that we would use it to move house. One home would halve the bills—the income from the proceeds of my mother's house would pay for much of her care. It would leave us in a more secure position financially to weather the storms of changing editors. If we all lived together in the south, I would be more accessible if my mother was taken ill and it would be easier to arrange her care. Three months would give us time to move, to get settled and to find a new team of helpers.

Frank wanted to move out of London; both of us like space, fresh air, the countryside and the sea. He wanted us to live near the River Blackwater in Essex where the boat is kept and where he had lived and his family still live. I had reservations. Although I love the country, I had lived in London for a long time. I liked its anonymity and its convenience for my work. I was apprehensive of living among Frank's relations.

The boat needed some structural work and it was arranged that we should have our summer holiday on Osea Island in the River Blackwater. Fabian, a shipwright and friend of Frank's who lives on Osea Island, would work on the boat. It would give us some rest, a chance to explore the area and to make up my mind.

I had thought of taking my mother to Osea Island but Frank protested and so did she. She shook her head and pointed smilingly at us.

136

"You think we ought to have a holiday on our own?" I queried.

She nodded vigorously. Once again, Gladys and Edna looked after my mother, this time helped by Anna and Mrs Bryant, a new lady. We had three weeks of bliss, wandering around the tiny island farm and sailing a dinghy to the hamlets and small towns along the shores of the river. We had to go to London to vote on election day and I spent it browsing through the shops and replenishing my depleted wardrobe. We sailed the dinghy to Maldon, a delightful little market town dating back to Roman times. We strolled along the quay, past the moored sailing barges through the clutter of Cook's boatyard and along the finger of colourful promenade. Like others before me, I started to fall in love with Essex.

By now, *Nursing Times'* new editor, Niall Dickson, had arrived. He was young and ambitious. While he seemed pleasant enough, I considered he had the makings of a typical whizzkid hatchetman, unconcerned about who or what he demolished on his way to the top. Like many of my colleagues, I regarded him with suspicion but I resolved to continue with my pattern of work and to wait and see what happened.

My mother's two sisters decided to visit and Aunt Alice came to stay in July. As a child I had spent many happy holidays with Aunt Alice and I am fond of her. She had had a long and happy marriage and my Uncle Jack had cossetted and adored her, reputedly leaving her a comfortably-off widow. She had no children and was regarded as having been too protected to give much practical help. She had not visited my mother since the trip to Ireland and I was apprehensive of how they might react to one another.

Her visit was a success. My mother was delighted to see her and Aunt Alice found little difficulty in communicating with her. Aunt Alice has an acute sense of humour and the two of them would play games accompanied by peals of laughter as Aunt Alice joked and poked fun. She would wheel my mother about and help her. As I watched them together, I thought what a good nurse Aunt Alice would have made. The weather was glorious and over the weekends Frank and I took them for picnics. During the week, Aunt Alice accompanied Gladys and my mother to the shops and all three enjoyed themselves.

As we kissed Aunt Alice goodbye in Liverpool airport, she said, "Let me know when your're moving. I'll come and help."

A few days later we received a touching thank-you letter and a cheque for £100.

In August, Aunt Emily arrived and I saw her twisted with emotion. To Aunt Emily, my mother was her eldest sister, a confidant and mentor from childhood days—she could not accept her helplessness.

"I miss you," she told my mother. "I used to tell you all my troubles and I knew I could rely on your advice."

I saw my mother struggle with her own emotions as she sat mute, the words locked from her lips. They had shared so much through words that they could find no substitute and it hurt them both deeply. Nothing I could do would help and we all knew when they parted that they were saying goodbye forever. They never saw each other again.

Recovery from stroke is a slow and gradual process. To outsiders my mother probably appeared unchanged but I was aware of small changes and achievements which made our lives happier. After her concentration improved, there would be a spurt of several small improvements followed by a period of months with no change and then another spurt. I noticed she had started to put away the dishes after meals and could arrange a bunch of flowers in a vase. She could manage to take off her shoes and socks, to paint or crayon a picture in different colours and to copy a few words accurately. She liked the telephone and, when relations or friends rang up, I gave it to her. I often spoke to her on the telephone when I was away.

Betty and Aunt Alice were particularly good at this and would prattle on unperturbed by my mother's response, "Do, da, do, da, do."

She had begun to enjoy some of the radio programmes again, particularly the church services and those with familiar characters such as the Archers. I was also able to have some quite complicated conversations with her and feel certain that I knew what she was telling me. We would talk about her stroke and her feelings about it or about religion or marriage. I sometimes read her pieces in which stroke victims described their feelings. She liked this and her responses told me much about her feelings. I admired her perseverance as she tried to overcome her handicap and to help in every way she could. She had an attractiveness and charm which people responded to and I saw her use and develop it. I often told her how much I admired her courage and sense of humour. I was grateful that the bouts of screaming had stopped and that she was so much easier to look after.

"You're so nice," I would say, "not cross and cranky like Granny was."

She was troubled with headaches and nosebleeds and once had two or three momentary blackouts. I was never certain that these were transitory and still found it difficult to leave her in case these heralded another stroke or some other major illness. I was keen to continue to reduce her drugs and we cut out the midday Merital capsule with no noticeable effect.

We had decided to start serious househunting in Essex. Our weekly commuting to see my mother was becoming more difficult as British Rail no longer allowed holders of cheap tickets to travel in the evenings before 6.30 pm. The result was that the trains were packed and we sometimes had to stand all the way. We arrived exhausted at my mother's house about 10.30 pm— late for my pensioner helpers to travel home. The fares had risen by more than 50% over the three years and we knew that travelling would become progressively more difficult and expensive. I longed for the day when we could stop travelling this two hundred miles or so but I also dreaded moving.

There was the trauma not only of moving house but also of setting up a complete new system of caring for my mother. I wondered how I would cope without Gladys. I had come to depend on her to take charge in my absence. Each week she organised the rota of helpers and doled out their pay packets which I left her. Gladys could be depended upon to cope with any emergency, calling the plumber when the lavatory cistern overflowed down the stairs and the doctor when my mother had a 'turn'. My mother and Gladys had become close friends and Gladys could handle her where others could not. My mother had regained her position as head of her household and supervised with the discipline of a martinet. While this was an achievement, it had its difficulties. For example one winter's night my mother refused to let Edna light the gas fire. It was bitterly cold but my mother was adamant. Edna finally rang Gladys who came round and persuaded my mother to relent.

I told Gladys that we had decided to start househunting. She agreed it was wise and offered to help.

"Your mother can come and stay with me while you move," she said.

"What will I do without you?" I asked her.

"You'll manage," she said. "Besides, John and I will come and look after your mother when you and Frank have your holidays."

I had not thought of that. It cheered me up.

One weekend in the middle of August, Gladys and Edna agreed to look after my mother while Frank and I went to househunt. As we kept the car up north, Ann lent us hers. We stayed in Maldon with Frank's sister Peggy and spent the entire weekend househunting. I soon realised that we would not be able to live in a village because it would be difficult to find help for my mother. We looked at ten houses and liked one which was too expensive but we made an offer. It was turned down. By Sunday we had exhausted the available possibilities. Frank started to work on the boat.

"I'll pop up to that first estate agent," I told him. "He might have something new".

The estate agent was showing a couple details of a bungalow.

"Can I see those details?" I asked when he had finished.

"It's not what you're looking for," he said.

I insisted and arranged to view it. I rushed back to the boat.

"Come on," I urged. "There's a bungalow just along the road overlooking the river."

It had been lived in by an old couple and had been standing empty for two years. The paint was faded and chipped in the spacious rooms, the ceilings were cracked and the boiler did not work. The overgrown garden stretched up a steep hill, the path blocked by intertwining braches of apple trees. I sat on the grass looking over the roof along the winding river, the peace broken only by the sound of birdsong. I wanted to live here; I knew my mother would like it. So did Frank.

The rigmarole and uncertainties of buying and selling began. We finally persuaded the agent to have the roof of our flat repaired. We spent our weekday evenings cleaning and painting it and we advertised it ourselves. Each weekend, Frank had to stay in London to show people around while I went north and worried in case the flat did not sell and we lost the bungalow.

I also faced the prospect of telling my mother about our plans and explaining that her house would have to be sold. I tried to explain that our present system was expensive and exhausting and that we would have to move and take her to live with us. She could not grasp it. Her understanding of money did not extend beyond the prices she saw in the shops. She had no idea where London or anywhere else was, or the time it took to travel. She could not understand why Frank and I could not move in with her. I explained about our need to work and the lack of suitable jobs or jobs of any kind in her area. It meant nothing to her. She did not want her house sold.

It upset me. I did not want to sell her house without her consent but we had no alternative. My mother had worked hard for her home and lived in it for almost a quarter of a century. It was her security and she loved it. I felt cruel to persist. I told her about the bungalow and took photographs so that she could see it. Nothing could sway her. I enlisted Gladys' help and, while I was away, she too would talk to my mother about it. In time she realised that the move was inevitable and she would have to accept it. She did, but sometimes she would protest and cry.

Moving is supposed to be one of life's most stressful events. I found it so. I was surrounded by emotional upheaval—my mother's distress, Frank's depression as the flat did not sell, and my helpers' worries that their jobs were coming to an end. I was afraid they might find other employment and leave before we were ready to move. We faced a good deal of work on the bungalow before it was fit to move my mother in and I had to pack up the flat and my mother's house. I wanted to keep my sabbatical leave to help us to get settled with new helpers so that much of the preparation had to be done while I was still working.

Once again I was becoming tired, worried and tense. The most frightening part was my inability to control my temper. I remember one weekend when Frank was in London.

I was ironing while my mother moaned, ''Do, da, do, da, do,'' continually in protest at moving.

I suddenly lost control, threw the iron and ironing board across the room, shouted, ''Shut-up,'' and screamed at the top of my voice.

My mother burst into tears. Fortunately the next-door neighbour ran in to see what had happened. I calmed down and made some feeble excuse which she clearly did not believe. Later I apologised to my mother and explained the pressures, reminding her of her own experience in Knockboy. Perhaps she thought it over. I noticed that she became more positive about the move and interested in our progress.

For all that, luck was now on our side. Niall Dickson, the new

141

editor of *Nursing Times*, did not turn out to be the ogre I had imagined. At first he wanted me to come into the office every day. I protested, explained my circumstances and the advantages to my job of first-hand experience at the receiving end of health services. He began to understand my strengths and difficulties and to my surprise he became interested. He would ask me searching questions others never thought of.

"But how do you know your mother understands?" he would persist. "How can you communicate with her?"

I enjoyed these talks with him as I struggled to explain the strange mixture of telepathy, gestures and intonation which took communication to a stage where my mother and I were unaware that she could not speak. Indeed I sometimes forgot to explain to strangers until I noticed their bewilderment. To help our move, Niall agreed that I could carry over a week's holiday into 1984 to move from the flat to the bungalow. My sabbatical leave could be taken in two six-week batches when we moved my mother.

On 7 November, Frank sold the flat to a cash buyer. There was no chain of buyers involved in either the bungalow or the flat. We were delayed only by legalities. As we decided it might take much longer to sell my mother's house, we asked a local estate agent to put it on the market. I told Mr Blundell, the bank manager, about our plans.

"If you get an offer, don't hang on for a higher price—sell," he advised me. "Property doesn't move here. You risk vandalism and lose money all the time it remains unsold."

It was good advice.

In the middle of November my mother nearly killed herself. Her upset over moving may have prompted nightmares or sleep-walking—I do not know. One night, without making a sound, she got out of bed and managed to move her wheelchair alongside and to get into it. She wheeled herself to the front door, removed the door mat, undid the chain bolt and Yale lock and pushed herself out. Her helper, sleeping upstairs, woke to the sound of my mother's shrieks as she tumbled down the steep steps into the garden. Her helper called an ambulance which came immediately and they carried my mother back to bed. Amazingly she was unhurt except for a few bruises and shock.

I wondered how she had managed this feat normally beyond her ability—she always needed help to move from bed to chair. I wondered how her helper could have slept through the noise of her moving which must have been transmitted through the baby alarm. A few nights later, when Frank and I were in the house, I woke to a strange crackling through the alarm and rushed downstairs to find her sitting on the edge of her bed. She seemed surprised and dazed. After this I rigged a handbell tied to a piece of tape which I pinned to the bedclothes after she went to bed. If she started to push the clothes back a loud clanging resounded throughout the house and through the baby alarm.

As a result of my mother's fall down the steps, our helper left, saying she could not face sleeping in the house again. While Gladys and Edna were old faithfuls, we had never had much luck with the third part-timer. None stayed more than three or four months and on one occasion the third helper had failed to turn up without letting us know that she had found another job. Fortunately Gladys and Edna never left my mother until relief had arrived and they filled the gap in this emergency. By now I had learnt a great deal about recruiting helpers. I kept a booklet with notes of every possible applicant who answered an advertisement. This reserve meant that a vacancy could usually be filled without re-advertising. It was a nuisance having to find another helper so soon before moving but we managed it.

We spent Christmas 1983 in my mother's home. I felt sad, knowing it was the last. The New Year would bring the final break with this home my mother and I had known for so long. I had also become fond of my mother's friends and neighbours and knew that I would miss them. I looked forward to living in the bungalow with some misgivings. Once we had moved there would be no escape—no two or three days' break in London each week. I wondered whether Frank would be able to tolerate living with my mother full time and, if he could not, what it would do to our marriage. I was incapable of making a choice between these two people I loved and to be forced into it might destroy me. I felt vulnerable, moving to a strange area away from my friends. I worried too about the layout of the bungalow which was divided by a long corridor separating the rooms so that it was impossible to hear from the kitchen what was going on in the sitting room. Innumerable snags and difficulties nagged in the back of my mind.

In January 1984 I took the promised week's holiday and we moved out of the flat and into the bungalow. Our meagre belongings made little impression on the bungalow, one room of which would have contained our whole flat. It was cold and empty; Frank, with the help of our next-door neighbour, set about getting the boiler going. I scrubbed and cleaned and we hired help with the painting. Frank's relatives rallied and cooked us supper each evening and by the end of the week the place was brightening up. In the middle of the week, Gladys rang to say that someone was making an offer for my mother's house.

To my amazement the sale started to go through. It was not without the usual hitches and uncertainties but go through it did and, even more astonishingly, to a first-time buyer not involved in a chain. I felt someone was on our side. To have three house transactions without a chain must be a good omen.

I arranged to take the first half of my sabbatical leave in the middle of March and move my mother. The intervening two months were exhausting. I spent the weeks commuting between my mother, London and Essex. Frank usually stayed in Maldon at the weekends to work on the bungalow while I spent them packing up my mother's home.

My mother joined in the packing. Together we sorted through drawers and shelves often getting lost in enjoyable reminiscences as we discovered long-forgotten items—my grandmother's scarf, a buckle from Great-Aunt Em's shoe, six 1930s hats my mother had bought for 1s. 6d. in Berwick Street market. My mother proved tougher than I was as she chucked bits and pieces into the waste-paper basket. I am a sentimental fool about things with old associations and found clearing out almost impossible. During the week, Gladys and my mother wrapped the china and dishes and packed them in cardboard boxes.

As moving day approached, Gladys and John converted their sitting room into a bedroom for my mother. It was decided that she should stay with them until we organised the move and prepared a room for her; then Gladys would take her on the train to London where we would meet them with the car. We booked their tickets and British Rail staff said they would ensure they had seats and arrange for my mother to be lifted on and off the train.

We fixed moving day for a Tuesday in the first week of my sabbatical leave. Frank and I spent the week-end beforehand finishing the packing and taking my mother to say goodbye to old friends. We had a last sad tea with Andy and Dorothy, and Alison and Jill, my mother's faithful friends from her babysitting days, came to say goodbye. On Monday afternoon we helped my mother into her coat and Gladys wheeled her away to her house. My mother shed a few tears but, as I watched them disappearing along the road, she never looked back. I wondered sadly how she felt, leaving her home for the last time. We had packed a small overnight bag for her and Gladys had hired a commode and bed cradle from the Red Cross so that all my mother's equipment could be transported in the removal van.

By Thursday morning, Frank and I and the contents of my mother's house were installed in the bungalow in Maldon although the place was in chaos. We had chosen a large bright bedroom overlooking the garden for my mother. I arranged her bed alongside the window and the rest of her bedroom furniture in much the same order as her old bedroom. I altered her curtains slightly to fit this window and when I had finished the room was not unlike the one she had left except it was larger, which enabled her to manoeuvre her wheelchair about the room and gave her access to all her clothes and personal things. Frank had fixed the baby alarm so that it could be switched on in our bedroom or the spare bedroom when we were away.

Gladys and my mother were arriving at Euston station, London, by early afternoon and it was a rush to be there on time. We arrived to find Gladys wheeling my mother along the platform, both of them smiling with the success of their adventure. We sat in the station snack bar drinking tea and Gladys described how they had been helped on and off the train and how much they had enjoyed the trip. We were reluctant to move as this was goodbye—Gladys was going back to clean my mother's house for its new owner. She was coming to spend a holiday in June but it was the end of the daily helping which had grown into a close friendship between Gladys and my mother. Frank finally urged us on and Gladys helped to pack the car. Now it really was goodbye and we were all weeping. We drove away, waving to a forlorn and tearful Gladys, my mother protesting— she wanted Gladys to come too.

We threaded our way through the London rush-hour traffic out into the Essex countryside, the river and our new home. It was dark long before we arrived and we had to wheel my mother into our home through our neighbour's drive. John and Joan had kindly offered to let us use it until such time as we could organise suitable access for a wheelchair.

My mother was tired but she wanted to see around.

"Do, da, do, da, do," she said approvingly as she looked around the large kitchen reminiscent of the farmhouses we knew with its red tiled floor and deal table.

She greeted her bedroom with cries of delight and surveyed the other rooms with enthusiasm as we navigated the wheelchair around boxes and tea chests.

"You'll be able to have a bath and sit on a proper lavatory again," I explained as we examined the bathroom.

My mother was delighted with her new home and later, as I helped her to bed following the familiar routine, I felt sure for the first time that we had made the right decision—everything would be all right.

10 Happiness

Wendy writes March 1984–June 1986

My mother settled in immediately. On the first morning she explored her room. I had replaced her clothes in the drawers in the same order they had always been in so it was easy for her to find everything. I thought this would encourage her to select her clothes each day—her previous bedroom had been too cramped for her to do this.

I encouraged her to move her wheelchair about the room saying, "You can move them yourself," when she indicated that she wanted some of her photographs and ornaments rearranged.

It took some time for her to work out exactly how to reach everything but, when she did, she was pleased with her achievement.

Next came the kitchen. We had bought an old deal kitchen table, large enough for four people but small enough to allow my mother to wheel her chair around the kitchen. There were plenty of cupboards which she could reach and she and I arranged the dishes and cutlery so that she would have no difficulty setting the table or putting away the dishes after a meal. Frank fixed accessible hooks on which she hung her apron and the tea cloths. She was now self-sufficient in carrying out her established jobs—setting the table, drying the dishes and putting them away after meals. Despite installing suitable aids, using the lavatory and having a bath or shower quickly palled. Within a couple of weeks she indicated that she preferred a commode in her room and her daily wash in the familiar way.

She took an interest in all the rooms, watching Frank and I change the furniture about or try a picture here and there to find the right place. She would join in, pointing where she thought things might fit or shaking her head if they looked wrong. She watched Frank building cupboards and shelves in the kitchen and examined them carefully, nodding approval or pointing out some fault she had spotted. She was enjoying herself. At last all three of us were building a future rather than patching up the past.

Aunt Alice had promised to help and she arrived a week after we moved in. By now my mother was familiar with the house and Aunt Alice helped by spending time with my mother, playing games, finding television programmes, helping her to move her wheelchair about and calling me if my mother needed the lavatory. Aunt Alice's presence enabled me to get on with other jobs without having to worry about my mother. She brought my mother a present of a brass handbell which would have been useful if my mother could have been persuaded to use it. She insisted on having it in her wheelchair and under her pillow at night but, whenever a difficulty arose, she failed to use it.

I advertised for a new team of helpers. We had a few replies. Unemployment in Maldon is low and it was to prove more difficult to find help, although not impossible. It took three advertisements to get a team together. After some juggling the rota ended up as follows.

Helper A: Monday, Tuesday and Thursday morning 8 am–2 pm when Frank and I were in London. 9 am–1 pm when I was working at home.

Helper B: Wednesday and Friday morning, same arrangement.

Two afternoon helpers: Only needed when I was in London. 2 pm–7 pm if Frank and I were in London. 3.30–5.30 pm if Frank was at home (to get my mother up from her afternoon sleep, to make tea, to have a game and to help her to the lavatory before leaving).

They were all paid at the local hourly domestic help rate. I kept a kitchen diary in which I noted as far ahead as possible the hours I needed help and pencilled the names of the helpers beside the hours. Each helper consulted the diary and ticked whether the hours suited her. This usually applied to the afternoon helpers as their days and times were less predictable.

The advantages of this rota were that it was flexible and all the helpers agreed to cover for each other for sickness and holidays. Part-time work is always popular and we knew that my mother liked this system. The disadvantages were that it was time-consuming to administer as each week's rota and weekly payments varied. I found that it ran more smoothly if I had an opportunity to talk to each helper during the week, which added another complication to organising the rota.

I started our first morning helper three weeks before I went back to work and the second morning helper a week beforehand. Both afternoon helpers came once or twice in the afternoon when Frank and I needed to go shopping. By the time I went back to work I was sure that both morning helpers could cope. My mother accepted all of them. Our two morning helpers stayed about six months. Our two afternoon helpers, Doreen and Aileen, stayed to the end of my mother's life. Doreen is a retired ward sister and Aileen a retired home help. Both became fond of my mother. They treated her as an old friend, often popping in at odd times to visit or bring her small gifts. She greeted them with pleasure and clearly enjoyed their company. Sometimes they would look after her on a Saturday or Sunday while Frank and I went for a sail.

With my return to work, a routine to suit our new life began to emerge. Fortunately neither Frank nor I travelled to London every day and we soon found it better to travel on different days. We needed to leave the house by 7.30 am to get to London on time and it was difficult to find helpers to start so early or to be on time. As I was unwilling to leave my mother alone until the helper had arrived, it was easier if one of us was in the house. If Frank was stuck, he could telephone one of the other helpers or, if all else failed, ask Joan, our next-door neighbour, to help in an emergency.

We were fortunate in having friendly and helpful neighbours who had come to welcome us as soon as we moved in. Joan and Joyce, another neighbour, had looked after the old lady who had owned our bungalow and they both helped us out in emergencies. Joan often wandered in during the morning and would sit and talk to my mother and have a cup of coffee with my mother and her helper.

On days when both Frank and I had to go to London, I waited until 8 am and caught a later train. Before I left the house I woke my mother, helped her onto the commode, settled her comfortably sitting up in bed and gave her tea. She usually slept again until her helper arrived, made her breakfast and got her up.

We usually arrived home about 7 pm. If Frank was at home; one of the afternoon helpers would come between 3.30 and 5.30 pm after which my mother would watch television—she enjoyed the early evening programmes. If she got fed up with them, she would push her chair into the bay window, watch the outside world and wave to me as I arrived home. This was her cue to set off down the corridor to the kitchen where Frank was preparing the evening meal and she would set the table.

We all enjoyed this part of the day. Sometimes, particularly if Frank and I had both been in London and came home tired, we would go out to eat. My mother enjoyed this enormously and we soon discovered which restaurants were accessible to a wheelchair and which welcomed us. We could get the wheelchair up steps but there were plenty of places with fixed tables and chairs, narrow doors or staff with scowling faces. Our favourites soon emerged—a local Chinese restaurant where we were greeted and helped enthusiastically, a pub where the landlord always helped get the wheelchair over the steps and a friendly hotel on special occasions.

My mother usually liked to go to bed about 9.30 pm and this took about half an hour or more. If I had to be away overnight, one of our helpers would come and assist my mother to bed. Frank usually coped alone at night unless my mother was having a 'waking phase' when I would try to get one of the helpers to sleep the night.

I asked everyone I met about the local doctors. We had to find a new doctor for my mother and I wanted someone who would be considerate and interested in her as well as someone from whom I could seek advice and trust. The difficulty about finding a new doctor is that it is only after you have signed on a doctor's list that you discover what he is like and what a dreadful mistake you have made. I soon found one doctor's name cropped up continually. Everyone seemed to recommend her and I decided to ask whether she would add us to her list.

The group's surgery was old fashioned and ill-equipped to cope with wheelchairs but Dr Booker was just what we needed.

She listened with interest to our story, added us to her list and promised to visit my mother every six weeks. My mother had enjoyed the small group arranged by the speech therapist in the north and I thought she might benefit from something similar in Maldon. Dr Booker suggested trying the day hospital once a week and she quickly arranged it.

On the first day Frank and I took her in the car. We wheeled her into the large room filled with activity. The staff were kind and helpful and thankfully there was no pop music. My mother sat with a small group at one of the tables. She looked lost and bewildered. I felt like a mother leaving her three-year-old on the first day at the play group. Still the place and the activity seemed pleasant and, when the ambulance delivered her home, she seemed quite pleased. She attended for about three weeks when she refused to go again.

I did not press her. Her days at home were filled with activity which she enjoyed. She had jobs which were her preserve and responsibility and which established her importance and contribution to our home. She had sufficient company and social exchange with the regular helpers and Joan next door. She could occupy herself for some part of the day with puzzles and jigsaws. Mary, one of the helpers, taught her to play clock patience which was a great success. She could move herself in her wheelchair from room to room and she could operate the television. When the weather was fine, she sat in the sun, dug the tubs in the garden or enjoyed walks by the river and along the promenade. At weekends we usually managed a drive or a marathon walk with Frank pushing the wheelchair. In the soft fruit season, we took her fruit picking. Best of all, she was clearly enjoying her life and this gave us pleasure.

We phased out the tranquilliser, Merital, not long after we moved to Maldon and it seemed that once completely off all drugs except her iron and vitamin C tablets, my mother was much better. She no longer screamed and cried. She was alert and smiling. It seemed to me as though she had travelled through some tortuous hell and come out enriched with some knowledge or certainty unavailable to the rest of us. She radiated a kind of joy which was more than a mere acceptance of her lot. I felt she had found something she had been searching for all her life and I knew too that having found it, she was prepared for death. She no longer feared it. Her radiance affected all of us. Our whole

She dug the tubs

house was filled with happiness and I marvelled daily at how this could have come about.

Gradually the pieces of our new life slotted into place. We found a new church which my mother liked and I was able to take her almost every week. I found a new bank manager, transferred my mother's account and invested the money from her house. We were given a rate rebate for having a disabled person living with us and we were given an extra grant to insulate the loft. As our heating depended on coal fires and an unreliable solid fuel boiler to heat the water, we had to make better arrangements before the winter. It was difficult to keep my mother warm even after we had installed central heating. Old people lose body heat through loss of body fat, brain damage or drugs such as tranquillisers or alcohol which can suppress the temperature control mechanism.

We took her fruit picking

It is easy for an inactive old person to develop hypothermia when the rest of the family are quite warm. In winter time I found the electric blanket by far the best preventer of cold. We would turn it on about an hour before my mother went to bed or lay down for an afternoon nap. By the time she got into bed it was beautifully warm and gradually heated her all over. In case of accidents I always switched it off once she was in bed. She wore several layers of wool—vest, light wool jumper and thick wool jumper or cardigan. Woollen trousers, woollie socks and sheepskin booties helped to keep her legs and feet warm. In winter her wheelchair was lined with a sheepskin cover and she sat on a duck-down cushion, easier on the bottom when sitting for much of the day. She kept a woollie rug over her knees. New light warm synthetic materials are now being developed which are especially useful for elderly people.

Despite all this we still had to watch out for cold. As typical of an old person with poor temperature control, she never complained of cold or shivered. A quick check is to feel that the skin under covered parts is warm to touch. If not, try to reheat the body gradually with more clothes and warm drinks. Sudden heat can be too much of a shock.

The summer heat could be almost as much of a difficulty as the winter cold. My mother enjoyed sitting in the sunshine but always wore a sunhat and after midday generally sat in one of the cooler rooms with the window open. Sunscreen cream and insect repellants helped to protect her delicate skin from burns and bites. She still suffered occasional small nosebleeds but these usually stopped by pinching the nose or lying down for a short time. She seldom caught colds but, when she did, she usually recovered fairly quickly. If she wanted to stay in bed, to prevent chest infection, we propped her in a sitting position and got her out in her wheelchair and into the kitchen for meals or to sit in her dressing-gown to watch television in the evening. A handkerchief and pillow regularly sprinkled with Olbas oil kept her air passages clear and allowed her to breathe more easily.

Some of her friends from the north came. Andy and Edna both stayed a week and Jill and Alison came for a day. Gladys often came, sometimes alone and sometimes with John. We all looked forward to Gladys' visits and my mother would greet her with renewed pleasure. The two of them would immediately slot into their old companionship and Gladys would push Frank and I off either for a long weekend or a holiday on the boat. When John came, we would insure our car for him to drive and he and Gladys took my mother on trips all over East Anglia. They ate jellied eels in Clacton and Southend, shopped in Basildon and Chelmsford, visited the zoo in Colchester and had cream teas in Burnham and Mersea.

I found myself much more relaxed and happy. Without the

John and Gladys took my mother on trips all over East Anglia

long tiring journeys back and forth, our weekends were longer and we had more time for outings or to work on our house. We bought a video recorder so that we could record my mother's favourite programmes and leave her to watch these if it was cold and we wanted to have a walk. I worried less about leaving her for an hour or so if I knew that she was engrossed in a film or a programme she enjoyed. We could usually get one of our helpers to sit for an evening if we wanted to go out. I found such arrangements an effort and, without Frank, I would not have bothered but, once we were away from the house, I always enjoyed myself and knew it was worth it.

Sometimes we invited people for supper. My mother always enjoyed this and would set the table carefully so that it looked attractive and welcoming. Some visitors were clearly uncertain how to react when they found my mother was part of the dinner party. I ignored this and carried on as usual. My mother had developed her own way of dealing with this—she would point out where they were to sit and act in a sort of quiet supervisory capacity, indicating when someone might need another helping or could not reach the sauce. My mother liked to go to bed at 9.30 pm and, when an opportunity arose, I would take her. She generally shook hands with everyone by way of saying goodnight and Frank would take over serving coffee while I was away.

I was always touched and pleased when a return invitation included my mother. She loved to be invited to other people's homes and some of our friends would go to endless trouble to see that her wheelchair could be fitted in. She no longer tried to catch the gist of a conversation between a group of people and somehow managed to be a non-participant without embarrassing anyone. One friend had a collection of beautiful antique glass and my mother always looked forward to examining these pieces. Sometimes she would sit and look at photograph albums or books of pictures.

We had been living in our new home about a year when my mother's brother Willie died in Ireland. He was a year older than my mother and had been the owner of Knockboy, the Irish family home. My mother and I had lived with him for many years and both of us were upset. I sat with her and held her hand, telling her that he had died. The tears rolled down her face. I hugged her, trying to comfort her. I knew what she was thinking.

I could almost see the thought, "I'm next," inside her head.

Over the next few weeks she spent a lot of time looking at photographs of him and, when Aunt Alice arrived for her holiday, I asked her to talk to her about old times, about their childhood and the forgotten faces in the faded photographs.

Aunt Alice's reminiscences provoked the two of them to gales of laughter. There were tales of illicit card games with the farm workers and booby-traps for posh town cousins who came to stay. There were wicked scheming aunts and benevolent uncles and school pranks. The two of them relived a microcosm of Irish rural life in the early part of the century to the exclusion of all else. It made them both happy and drew them closer together.

Aunt Alice had been to see her doctor who was treating her for high blood pressure. She did not seem as well as she had been and one day she collapsed in the kitchen. I called the doctor who came almost immediately and, as Aunt Alice recovered, we found out what was wrong. It seemed she had been given tablets to reduce her blood pressure. She was supposed to take one in the morning and one at night but she was so frightened of forgetting the second tablet that she had taken it at lunch-time which pushed her blood pressure so low that she collapsed. Once the importance of the timing was explained, she promised not to do this again. Next day I bought her a present of a pill-box with three compartments so that she could measure out her tablets each day, marking each compartment with the time they were to be taken. This helped to prevent any muddles about whether or not the tablets had or had not been taken.

I thought she needed some help at home but she told me that the home help organiser had been to see her but could offer nothing. Aunt Alice enjoyed the company of my mother's helpers and I knew she would like someone similar to come in for a couple of hours a few times each week. She could easily afford it.

"Did you ask the home help organiser whether she knew any retired home helps who might come to you privately?" I enquired.

"Yes," she said. "You told me to do that but she said they don't have anything to do with private arrangements."

I felt irritated. It was typical tunnel-vision bureaucracy. It was not the organiser's fault that she did not have enough helps to go round but why not try to help people to help themselves?

I wrote a couple of little postcards advertising for help and gave them to Aunt Alice.

"Put them in the local shops," I told her. "You'll get someone or, if you don't, try the local paper."

She kept them for a day or two and then handed them back.

"I can't do it," she said. "I'm an old woman. I can't risk inviting a stranger into my home to interview them."

She was right. She was stuck without help but, if someone had a list of vetted helps or were prepared to help her to interview, she could have had the help she wanted.

I was worried about what arrangements to make if my mother died. Before her stroke and before I married Frank, she had arranged to be buried in the family grave in Ireland. I saw this fraught with difficulties and I wondered whether she still wanted this but it was difficult to broach the subject. It nagged and nagged in my mind and one day while we were sitting together at the kitchen table I plucked up courage.

"Frank and I have been talking about being buried," I said. "I doubt whether we'll move anywhere else and he and I are going to be buried in the cemetery here. Would you like to be buried with us or go back to Ireland?" I asked.

My mother seized my hand, the tears streaming down her face.

"Do, da, do, da, do," she said with such thankfulness and relief that I knew that it had bothered her too.

There was no doubt. She made it clear that she wanted to stay with Frank and me. I promised to show her the cemetery and a few days later I did.

After that, whenever we passed it in the car, she pointed out happily saying, "Do, da, do, da, do," which I took to mean that she was pleased with the arrangement.

In August 1985 my mother was eighty and I decided to have a special party. Chantek, Frank's daughter, agreed to make a cake and somehow or other she managed to cover it with eighty candles. I invited the friends my mother had made in Maldon. They included Peggy, Frank's sister and Lorna, his sister-in-law Liz, his niece and her children. My mother's helpers Mary, Doreen, Aileen and Irene, John and Joan next door, Tom, who sometimes helped to dig the garden and liked a game of draughts, his wife Betty, and Butts and Enid who keep the pub on the quay and always had a special welcome for my mother.

I had arranged the party for 3.30 pm and, while my mother had an afternoon nap on her bed, Aunt Alice and I prepared the food and the table. What a success—everyone brought small gifts and cards and my mother was the centre of attention. Everyone helped to blow out the candles and we took lots of photographs so that my mother could relive the day time and time again. As we cleared away, I felt strangely sad. Something told me it would never happen again.

In the five years since my mother's stroke the plight of elderly dependent people and their carers has attracted more publicity. Everyone recognises that old people prefer to be looked after in their own homes. It has become government policy to promote 'community care', and long-stay hospitals for the mentally ill and mentally handicapped are discharging their patients and closing while acute hospitals are pushing patients out as quickly as possible. Most of this 'community care' means that wives and daughters must devote their lives to the dependants. They have little support as local authorities find their rate support grants reduced and direct their stretched and meagre services to unsupported old people living alone.

To reduce demand on hospital beds, the government has introduced DHSS support for low-income old people to live in nursing homes. This encourages their use as local authorities grasp this straw to escape increasing demand and relatives find they cannot cope without support at home. This often happens because women have to give up their jobs and to use the attendance allowance to compensate rather than to buy the relief they need. In 1985, Mrs Jackie Drake had still to win her case in the European Court of Justice which made the weekly Invalid Care Allowance available to married as well as to single women.

Nursing Times was taking an interest in carers and one day the topic was raised at an editorial meeting. I sat silent as the discussion ranged over the horrific plight of carers left for years without holidays or even a few hours' break from their twenty-four-hour round. No one paid attention to me. Eventually I chipped in.

"I'm a carer," I volunteered.

All eyes turned on me. There was a pause.

"But you're not a real carer," someone said. "You have a job and you get other people to do the work."

I was flabbergasted. I thought of the hours of planning, advertising, interviewing, demonstrating and supervising, the

159

nagging worry that never left me away from home and the effort involved in arranging every outing and trip. I thought of the hours of work before and after I left the office, the disturbed nights and the emotional juggling to keep my marriage, my job and my mother on an even keel.

"I suppose I'm not," I replied weakly, but the remark stayed with me—"You're not a real carer."

The more I thought about it the more I began to realise what was wrong. Attention is not focused on the reasons why some people manage and the arrangements they make. Nobody explores their success and tries to transfer these ideas to the less fortunate. Instead, professionals, editors and journalists focus on the horror stories and demand more resources for statutory services which are often too inflexible to meet individual circumstances.

All around me I see interesting initiatives. I know two retired nurses who offer a respite service. They will live in the dependant's home while the carer has a weekend off or a holiday. They never advertise but the demand far outstrips anything they can provide. Co-operatives provide some innovative and flexible caring arrangements in Europe, and in Britain the co-operative movement is growing. In Sunderland, one provides a popular home help service. Each time I advertised for help I had a crop of replies from the newly retired looking for part-time employment. Many had relevant expertise in health or social services or even better had been or were carers themselves. But who is tapping into this? Who is encouraging it or putting carers and helpers in touch with one another? Health and social services regard it as outside their province and the Manpower Services Commission and local enterprise boards ignore it.

Companies such as Marks and Spencer offer their retired employees a welfare service but there is no incentive from government or other companies to follow suit or to explore other possibilities, nor is there any encouragement for employers to give carers consideration similar to pregnant mothers—the leave to make arrangements or move to part-time work.

Now reports and recommendations from Age Concern, the British Medical Association and the DHSS are appearing. I have written about many of these in *Nursing Times* and, when the Cumberlege report on community nursing services was published, I was encouraged by a colleague to write about our

160

situation. I felt I could not write without my mother's agreement. I told her what I was doing and read out the relevant copy. She smiled at me and nodded.

"One day I'll write a book about it all. Would that upset you?" I asked.

She grimaced, thought about it for a while and then grasped my arm and shook her head.

"You'd like me to write about it?" I queried.

She nodded vigorously and we sat a while talking of what to write about—her coping experiences and mine. When the photographer came to take pictures for the *Nursing Times* article, she co-operated happily and we admired the results together.

During the late autumn I began to notice that my mother seemed less robust. She ate less and I chided her until one day she vomited her food, spotted with fresh blood. I showed it to the doctor. She could find nothing wrong. The next step was hospitals and tests. My mother gripped my arm and shook her head. I knew she wanted no more hospitals. She was happy here with us and she wanted to be with us until she died. If this was her death knell, she had no wish to postpone the day.

The days drifted by towards Christmas. My mother rejected more and more solid food and I began to purée everything. She could manage her tea and porridge in the morning. Mid-morning I substituted Build-Up, one of the several fortified powders which when added to milk makes a pleasant easily digested nourishing drink. Lunch was usually liquidised soup made from chicken and fresh vegetables. When she could no longer eat even steamed white fish, her evening meal consisted of milky fruit drinks made from warm milk beaten up with a raw egg, two teaspoonfuls of sugar and half a banana, an orange or blackcurrants. When we all went out for a celebratory Christmas meal, she enjoyed the occasion but only had soup.

Apart from being unable to manage solid food, her life went on as usual. On Christmas Eve she wanted to go to the midnight service. She slept on her bed in the evening and I woke her at 11 pm. Well wrapped against the crisp December air, Frank and I wheeled her to All Saints' Church. As usual, she sat in the front of this lovely old church, candlelit and packed with people for this traditional service. It was a splendid and moving occasion. When it was over, we sat and listened to the organ until the crowds had thinned. As we left, Canon Dunlop, now a familiar friend, kissed her hand and blessed her for Christmas. In January it was too cold to go out and church was replaced by the television Sunday service.

My mother lost weight and I was surprised how alert and active she remained. Occasionally she would vomit for no apparent reason and once again I would suggest investigation. She would hold my hand and smile, shaking her head. Each time the doctor visited she would turn to me fearful and questioning.

Each time the doctor and I reassured her, "It's only a check. There won't be any hospital."

She was content and happy. It is one of the blessings of old age that the elderly seldom feel pain—she had none. In the afternoons she would lie still and quiet on her bed, watching the birds cluster on the string of nuts that hung outside her window. She would wake each morning and greet me with a glorious smile.

"Do, —— da, do, da, do," she would say in pleased surprise as though to say, "How lovely. I'm still here. I've been given another day."

As she grew more frail, her helpers cosseted her, fearful almost that she would break when they touched her. Mary, our chief morning helper, had developed a very close relationship with my mother and was particularly worried about her. My mother, who loved Mary and her quiet peaceful calm, would put a reassuring hand on Mary's arm.

"Do, da, do, da, do," she'd say, telling her not to be sad or worry.

I dreaded what might be ahead of us. I remembered my grandmother, the last eighteen months of her life spent bedridden, helpless and almost unconscious. I resented Frank's appeals to come sailing as the weather grew warmer. I wanted to stay with my mother.

"We have the rest of our lives to go sailing," I would say. "When my mother dies, we'll never see her again."

"She'll never die," he would say. "She'll go on for ever."

He always regretted the words, spoken in haste, but they hurt me. I did not want my mother to die but at the same time I knew it was inevitable. I wanted to be with her and to help her in whatever way I could to die in dignity and comfort with love and peace around her. I was also aware that Frank felt that the time when he could enjoy the physical demands of sailing was ebbing

162

away. There were others he could take sailing but he wanted only me. I felt torn to pieces.

Since our move we were more financially secure and I would have liked to work part time. I tried to avoid travelling long distances or being away over night and I felt badly about it. Niall was sympathetic but he did not like the idea of part time.

"If your mother is ill and you need extra time, don't worry; we'll sort it out," he said.

I noticed my mother sleeping more and the physical exertion of her daily walk down the passage with her tripod and moving her wheelchair tired her out. She persisted in tackling her household jobs but was often pleased to be let off.

"You deserve a rest," I would say. "I'll dry the dishes tonight."

She continued to enjoy her games but a two-hour television film was too long. I recorded shorter, less demanding pieces which she could watch when she felt like it. Walks too were shorter—a half-hour gentle stroll in the wheelchair in the May sunshine was long enough. The effort of attending church became too much and instead Canon Dunlop came once a month to give her communion.

My mother's favourite Bible readings were Psalm 23 'The Lord is my Shepherd' and Psalm 121 'I will lift up mine eyes unto the hills'. Now she wanted me to read one or other each night as though it might be her last. In June, Aunt Alice came. We took them both for a short drive to the sea. It was a glorious sunny day and my mother wanted to go. I was doubtful and it proved almost too much for her. She came back exhausted. Aunt Alice sat with her and stayed by her side each day. As the June days drifted lazily away, the sisters seemed to draw even closer together.

We had arranged our holiday for July, and Gladys and John had arranged theirs to coincide so that they could look after my mother while we were away. Our helpers too had fixed their arrangements and it would have been difficult to unscramble anything but I was reluctant to go. We abandoned the first week of it, and Gladys and I both looked after my mother. She was getting up each day and would sit in her wheelchair for a couple of hours. She still enjoyed a game and insisted on drying the dishes now and then. In the evenings she liked to watch Emmerdale Farm on the television. After two hours in her wheelchair she would want to lie down and we would alternate her periods of sitting in her wheelchair with naps on her bed, on

163

the sitting room settee, on a recliner in the garden or in a reclining armchair in the window overlooking the river. The regular changes of place and position gave some variety to her day and helped to prevent her buttocks from getting sore. Her skin was very frail and thin but this regime prevented it from breaking.

By now she found even liquidised food or a whole packet of Build-Up in milk too difficult to swallow. She could not swallow tablets and we gave her liquid iron instead. She was living on two-hourly cups of warm milk sweetened with three teaspoons of glucose and a teaspoon of Build-Up. She had sufficient fluid to keep her mouth moist and her kidneys working. Rectal suppositories administered every three days avoided having to take a laxative and kept her bowels working. A glycothymol mouthwash morning and evening kept her mouth clean and fresh.

When Gladys had been with us a week, she seemed suddenly to be getting better. Now she was worried that we were not having our own holiday. Eventually it was decided that we would have a week on the boat locally and telephone every day. I was reluctant to go but she seemed to want it and everyone presented arguments as to why I should go. I wished the holiday would go away. She grasped my hand and smiled at me when I asked if it would be all right.

"I'll ring every evening," I told her. "Gladys will ask you if you want me to come home—promise me you'll let her know."

She nodded, smiling, almost pushing me towards the door.

I left heart heavy, eyes burning and comforting myself by asking, "We've been expecting it since Christmas, why should she die while I'm away?"

164

11 Landfall

Frank writes October 1983–June 1986

Our bungalow has a crack in its foundation; otherwise we would never have been able to buy it. You can see the crack zigzagging up the brickwork on each of the side walls and snaking across the ceilings.

"It's been there for at least twenty years," our neighbour John said the first day we saw it, "and it's got no worse."

Mortgage companies, of course, could never be persuaded to take a hopeful, optimistic view of a good crack and had always shied off. Consequently, because we would buy the house without a mortgage, I was able to grind the poor vendor down to a figure we could afford. What we got for Wendy's tiny flat in London almost paid for our bungalow, a spacious place in a lovely spot with a lovely view over the head of the estuary. When my old friend Keith and his uncle brought our furniture from London, he could not believe that the two places had an almost equal value.

"What," he said, "swop this shoe box for a lovely bungalow? I should say so."

I laid *Iskra* up, thankful to be home after her travels I believe, her mud berth, as it happens, at the end of the road we now live in. I did not know this when I put her away in mothballs until such time as we would be able to take her away on another voyage. Getting *Iskra* safely home and safely laid up allowed me to concentrate my mind and my energy on the business of living and looking after Adeline which, so far, Wendy had borne the brunt of. It was Wendy who first saw the bungalow and recognised its value to us. I took one look at it and knew at once that we would be happy in it. To Adeline, it was a return to Torquay, to her youth and to the middle-class life she had forsaken—she had come home to rest, all her fears for herself and Wendy at rest as well.

There was a blessed release of tension as soon as we were all under one roof and the almost schizophrenic divisions of locality at an end. Either the feeling of serenity which we all enjoyed or the fact that Wendy had weaned Adeline off all drugs had a profound effect on her. The screaming and shouting were gone; a benign good humour suffused her personality. If it had not been for Wendy, Adeline would not have been taken off the drugs at all. It seems that a doctor, having prescribed a drug, will leave the patient to continue it regardless of whether it is doing what it is supposed to do and regardless of what other thing it is doing which it is not supposed to do. It is open to question whether any of the drugs prescribed for Adeline ever did her any good whatsoever. For a long time I had harboured the notion that Adeline would outlive me or, worse, would outlive Wendy—it had played on my mind when I had been alone in the ocean. Now this fear gradually left me as I began to accept our way of life.

In a curious way, looking after Adeline drew Wendy and me together as nothing else could have done. We are both immeasurably richer for the experience of looking after her. She taught us how to give and she taught us how to accept love. I began by respecting her, even fearing her as she was before her stroke. I came to resent her, to be frustrated by her, sometimes to hate her and at best to be sorry for her. I ended by loving her, not as Wendy loved her with that strangely intimate relationship between a daughter and her mother, which no man can fully understand or imitate, but as someone who gave love to me and made me able to receive it. I still believe that I was right to oppose the blood transfusion but at the same time I am aware that, if I had been successful in my opposition and Adeline had died at that time, I would have missed the wonderful experience of being with her for the last year of her life. This is an enigma I cannot pretend to resolve.

We included Adeline in everything we did. We exchanged Wendy's Mini for a Mini Estate which the wheelchair and all our gear would easily go in. We took her on wonderful country walks, pushing her through cornfields, over stiles, along the sea wall, down to the shore at Bradwell where *Iskra* is kept in the

166

summer, out to the end of the promenade at Maldon and along the quay where the barges lie. She would watch me working on the boat gear and I would give her little jobs to do. She had a beady eye for detail and would spot holidays in the paintwork or forgotten bits. She would never allow us to go out and forget to turn off the light or to lock the door or to forget anything we needed.

She became something of a cult figure in Maldon, saying, 'Da, do, da, do, da, do,'' to her friends and acquaintances in a dignified, almost regal fashion as we wheeled her through the streets.

When we were away and Gladys and John took her out in the town, people would stop and talk to them because they knew Adeline. She was given a position for her wheelchair in the very front of the church, the vicar giving her his special blessing. When we took her to the pub—she would never have been seen within a mile of a pub before her stroke—the landlord would come to the door and help to lift the wheelchair over the step and clear a passage through the bar to her special seat by the window overlooking the river. Her emancipation never led quite as far as a glass of strong drink.

Once the routine was firmly established in the pattern Wendy had devised, the system performed smoothly. The ladies came and went at their appointed times, they brought home-made cakes and, when Wendy was in London, we would sit round the kitchen table and hold hilarious tea parties. There were great jam-making sessions, Adeline assisting the process with gusto. She minced the marmalade oranges until she and everything around her was covered in marmalade, roaring with laughter at the fun of it and sticky from her fingers to her eyelashes. In a short time we established helpers who liked Adeline and who we liked—they are our friends still. I used to spend hours looking after her myself; she would sit doing her puzzles or watching television while I worked. The only thing I could not do for her, except in a dire emergency, was to put her on the lavatory—this offended her natural modesty deeply.

Adeline could be left in the house by herself, as she frequently was, provided that someone came to do things for her which she was unable to do for herself. Wendy's system was far nicer for her than any nursing home would have been and she responded, as people do respond to kindness, by being nicer herself. It was also

Sticky with marmalade from fingers to eyelashes

considerably cheaper than a nursing home. It enabled Wendy to keep her job, which was fundamental to our way of life, and it enabled us to preserve Adeline's small capital intact instead of being forced to use her assets to pay for a nursing home.

If both of us had been in jobs that kept us away from home for eight or ten hours every day, it would have been difficult but not impossible, given some constructive help from the social services. Adeline was helpless, but an old person who can to some extent fend for himself can often live at home, with help. One of our ladies, following Wendy's example, kept her old father in his house until he died with great advantage both to the old man and to his family. If the enormous sums spent by the state in financing old people in private nursing homes were to be channelled into the social services, Wendy's system would become commonplace.

Looking after Adeline was not always a smooth and easy business. The following is a quotation from an article I wrote in *The Guardian* newspaper in February 1985:

'Wendy had to go to a conference in Manchester, before Christmas when there was snow on the ground, leaving me in charge. The first day I give Adeline tea in the morning, pull her up in bed, adjust the cushions and clothes around her neck and say a few kind words.

She beams at me, "Da, do, da, do, . . .," she says.

The first lady comes at nine and puts her on the commode—I am not sorry that Adeline's delicacy of feeling relieves me of this task.

She is breakfasted, washed, dressed and put in her wheelchair. She dries the breakfast dishes, wheels herself about our bungalow, lays the table, polishes furniture and does her puzzles on the kitchen table. I work in the study. The first lady gives her lunch, puts her to bed for an afternoon rest and waves goodbye. I go to the pub along the road for half a bitter. It is snowing.

I get Adeline up from rest—"Da, do, da, do," she says as I come into her bedroom.

I sit her up, swing her legs round and onto the floor as taught by Wendy, position the wheelchair beside the bed on my right, stand facing her, legs apart, put my right arm round her waist—careful of the paralysed shoulder—and lift. She is able to stand, unsteadily on one leg. I turn her through ninety degrees and plonk her down in the wheelchair.

"Da, do, da, do," she says.

I am sweating. It is snowing harder.

The second lady is due at four. It is snowing harder still—she does not turn up. I phone. Her car is stuck—she is so sorry. It is getting near to commode time—Adeline is in the drawing room, her tray fixed to her wheelchair.

I used to hate her because she was ruining our lives. I used to wish she would die.

At first, when she was on drugs, she was impossible—screaming and shouting, "Da, do" at the top of her voice, driving Wendy into the ground and driving a wedge between us.

I thought she was a narrow, bigoted old woman; I thought it was a travesty of common sense to keep her alive with drugs.

Wendy stuck it out and would not send her to a home because she knew they would be cruel to her—not because they wanted to be cruel but because Adeline cannot speak, and cannot tell them what she wants. Adeline had devoted her life to Wendy—Wendy could not let her die unhappy.

I telephone the third lady and she says she will come at once—Adeline is saying, "Da, do" apprehensively.

Soon she comes, bravely trudging through the snow. She is a new lady—has only once been shown how to get Adeline out of the chair, pants down, onto the commode and back again, pants up.

"I'll manage," she says.

The snow comes thicker. I go out for supplies while I still can. When I come back, all is confusion.

The third lady has tried to put Adeline on the commode and failed—Adeline nearly fell, lost her balance, and her nerve, and has begun to shout.

"Da, do, da, do, da, do."

I say, "Come on—it's got to be done. I'm going to help her."

She looks at me and nods her head dubiously. We position the commode, the chair at right-angles. I lift Adeline, hold her precariously and turn her, the lady pulls down her pants—plonk on the commode—sighs of relief, hissing noise, reverse procedure.

Adeline looks at me, smiles and chuckles, "Do, da, do, da, do."

She still has a sense of humour. The fourth lady comes at bedtime, puts Adeline on the commode and tucks her up for the night.

Now I do not want her to die any more. She has taught us to do things we thought we could not do. She has taught us about caring, about giving and about receiving. She has turned our lives upside down and has stopped us from doing what we want to do but it has been worth it and it still is. I do not hate her any more—I love her.'

170

The system usually ran itself; it became a routine which we hardly thought about. After a year at the bungalow I decided to fit out *Iskra* again. Wendy encouraged me in this, partly because she loves the time we spend together in the boat, partly to demonstrate the smooth running of her system and partly because she felt in some way responsible for her mother's plight and always tried to mitigate its effect on me.

One day, when we were in the pub with Adeline, I met an Icelander called Berent who persuaded me that a voyage to his country would be propitious.

"It's not too far for you," he said. "You can be there and back inside a summer and we'll look after you well."

Under the influence of a pint or so and Berent's bonhomie I readily agreed. Berent went back to Iceland and I promptly forgot the commitment until a few weeks later when a long rolled-up parcel arrived at the bungalow with a strange stamp and postmark. It contained the navigation charts for Iceland. We spread them out on the floor and Wendy and I pored over them and wondered how it could be managed.

We did manage, this time without pain or trauma for Adeline. I took *Iskra* to Iceland, Gladys and John came to stay in the bungalow, and Wendy came out by aeroplane and joined me in Reykjavik. Together we took *Iskra* round the north of Iceland, way up into the Arctic Circle, along the tortuous, convoluted coastline to Akureyri. Wendy flew back home and I brought *Iskra* back to Maldon as I had from America; only this time it was a shorter, easier journey. It was the first holiday we had had that Wendy felt no worries about Adeline. Her worry—Wendy is a person who finds it necessary always to have something to worry about—was for ourselves. She took a look at Iceland, first the moonscape topography of the land and then the jagged, rock-strewn coastline and immediately wrote a new will and posted it to her solicitor in London. It turned out not to be necessary.

Adeline gave us all ample notice of her impending demise. Slowly but with an inevitable daily progression she began to get weaker and frailer. Yet her will remained as inflexible as ever. It was as if she had planned her death and was determined to stick to the itinerary. Gladys and John came to stay for their summer holiday; Adeline knew that this was the signal for us to go away. She insisted that we went and we did go, after a false start when I persuaded Wendy that we should not and we went back. In the end, Adeline almost drove us out of the house and we left her for ten days. We did not go far; Wendy telephoned every day, and sometimes twice. When we came back, it was clear she had decided that her time had come.

Adeline became thin, and her skin took on a transparent quality, quite beautiful in its way. She sat for hour on hour in her wheelchair, gazing out of the window, listless and inert, her thoughts an unsolvable mystery to us and perhaps to herself. It was as good a way to end her life as she could have hoped for. It had been a life with few pleasantries, few of the heights of enjoyment that most of us can look back on in our decline, and few of the fruits of her unremitting labour. In real terms her achievement was marathonic. She left Torquay with Wendy in her arms and £50 her total wealth. She came to buy her own house, paid for out of her minute earnings without the aid of a mortgage. She retained her sense of humour to the end. Her life was no round of fun in the conventional sense; the fun was deep within her and in this respect at least she was her own daughter's mother. One bounty she had which perhaps made up for the dearth of delight—Wendy's love, given to her with unhesitant willingness and unstinting generosity.

12 Journey's End

Wendy writes July 1986 and after

We came back on Friday afternoon. Each evening I had telephoned Gladys and asked my mother whether she wanted us to come back from holiday.

Each evening the answer was, "No."

Now she opened her eyes and smiled, reaching out her hand to me as I sat on the edge of her bed. I felt shocked at how thin and weak she looked. It was always a shock to come back bursting with things to say—her lack of speech jolted me anew.

On Saturday, John went home and Gladys went shopping. I helped my mother to wash and dress and sat beside her as she lay on the recliner in the sunshine. The birds sang and flitted around us and, fanned by a gentle breeze, she nodded off under the sunshade.

On Sunday night she watched television for a while but at bedtime she seemed unable to help herself, and Gladys and I lifted her into bed. I got up several times in the night to turn her and to keep the pressure off her tender skin. Reluctantly Gladys went home on Monday and I rang *Nursing Times* office.

"I must stay here," I said. "She's too ill to leave."

She drank a little milk but it was an effort to drink from a cup. Frank borrowed a feeding cup from the Red Cross. I took the sheepskin off her wheelchair and put it under her bottom, tying it to the bed so that it did not wrinkle. Sheepskin helps to prevent the skin from becoming sore but this one was rather small. I rang the surgery and asked whether the doctor could visit and whether we could borrow a ripple mattress or large sheepskin. Her skin was so thin and stretched that I felt it could break at any

173

time. Doreen called in and helped me to wash her, to change her nightie and to make her comfortable.

She slept most of the day, refusing everything but a few sips of glucose and water. I sat by her bed. The sun shone; the breeze lifted the curtains. A doctor from the surgery came and went. The district nurse came to say there were no ripple mattresses but she would order a sheepskin—the bureaucracy was slow and cumbersome and I was glad we had our own sheepskin, however inadequate.

Tuesday drifted by, punctuated by two-hourly turning and sips of fluid. She was so light I could turn her and lift her onto the commode myself. In the afternoon she woke up quite alert.

"Would you like to lie on the settee for a while?" I asked.

She smiled and nodded and I helped her into the wheelchair. She slept propped up with numerous cushions on the settee in the sitting room. I stayed with her until Frank came home. She held out her hand to him.

"Do, da, do, da, do," she greeted him weakly.

"Will you be all right here while I make supper?" I asked.

She nodded, smiling and drifted back to sleep. At 9 pm I helped her to bed. She followed her routine exactly, even checking to see that the brakes were secured on her wheelchair. I noticed her breathing was shallower. It became more laboured and at 10 pm I called the doctor. He—a new doctor I had not met—came straight away. He examined my mother and I led him into the sitting room.

"I think she may have had another stroke on Sunday," he told me. "She has pneumonia and not long to go, I'm afraid."

Anything he could do to ease her breathing might make her more uncomfortable in other ways.

I went back and sat on her bed, holding her upright against me to ease her laboured breathing. Frank came in.

"Open the windows wide to get some air," I asked, and the warm July night breeze swept in.

"Don't fight it," I begged her, uncertain whether she could still hear me.

As if in response, she stopped breathing and lay quietly against me while her life ebbed away.

Frank telephoned the doctor to tell him she had died. He came back shortly after midnight and sat with Frank and me on her bed.

"I wish I'd known her," he said to me.

I began to tell him about her. Frank joined in. We showed him the photographs the *Nursing Times* photographer had taken a few months before. The doctor listened, prompting us with questions. We spent an hour together gathered around her, reminiscing and reliving happy moments of our time together. I felt that her spirit was with us. There was no unhappiness. I was sure this was how death ought to be. This gentle doctor, who must have been tired, helped me to straighten her body and to leave her in rest and peace before he left.

"I'm glad that you can talk about it," he told me. "Try to get some sleep."

Then he turned to Frank, "I'll have a death certificate at the surgery in the morning."

In the night I got up and went into the sitting room. I sat in the place where she had slept that evening. I clung to the cushions that seemed to hold some last essence of her. I wept for the loss of her. I did not wish her back in her worn-out body but I wept for the strong, courageous spirit that had been my mother. I watched the dawn rise over the river on the first day of a world without Adeline in eighty-one years. It was ten days before her birthday. I wondered what my grandmother had been doing and feeling, waiting for Adeline to arrive eighty-one years ago. I wished I had a daughter—a new, strong, young Adeline.

When it was daylight, I took warm water and towels into her room. I washed her and laid her body out as I had learned long ago in hospital. I dressed her in a favourite nightie.

"Do, da, do, da, do," she used to say delightedly whenever it appeared.

It was the last care that I could give her and they were the last quiet moments we spent together. I said goodbye to her.

I wanted to keep her body in the house but the undertaker said the weather was too hot. She was taken away and I was swept along in a tide of arrangements and activity. Later I wished I had investigated funeral arrangements and cemeteries thoroughly beforehand. I loathed the funeral parlour's plastic flowers and piped music. I poured out my heart to Canon Dunlop and he arranged for my mother to lie in front of the altar of the beautiful, peaceful church my mother had loved.

There were letters and flowers from relatives, friends, neighbours and *Nursing Times*. Canon Dunlop took her funeral service and we buried her in Maldon cemetery. The little knot of people trickled back to the house for tea—Aunt Alice, cousins Harry and Niall, Gladys, Frank's relatives, Tom who digs the garden, Joan and John next door, Canon Dunlop and my mother's helpers Mary, Irene, Doreen and Aileen. As I said goodbye to my mother's helpers, I knew I would miss them. How silent and quiet the house would be.

"It wasn't like a job," said Mary. "It was such a happy home I'll miss coming here."

"I learnt a lot from your mother," said Aileen. "She was a great brave lady."

I felt none of the paralysing grief I had felt when she had had her stroke. I simply missed her—no smiling face watching from the window for me, no place at the table, no wheelchair coming along the passage, no rapturous "Do, da, do, da, do", no help to dry the dishes, no finger pointing to the forgotten cake in the oven, no chats in the bathroom at the weekend when I washed her and no sounds of busy activity or laughter—just silence everywhere. Friends offered to clear her room. I declined and left it as it was. Sometimes I sit in there, comforted by her presence which I feel around me.

We decided to mark her grave with a simple wooden cross—Frank wanted to make it. The local council refused permission. We did not pursue it—her memory is too precious, and too fragile to mar with strife or bitterness. She needs no regulation off-the-peg stone monument. She built a unique and priceless one in the hearts of those who knew her.

As I write, almost a year has passed since she died. I begin to feel less tired. It surprised me how long the feeling of exhaustion persisted. It was several weeks before I got used to leaving the house without making arrangements for someone to relieve me. I think of her every day but she is seldom in a wheelchair. She is serene and younger. She walks and talks. It was a strange, unforeseen journey that Frank, my mother and I travelled in those last six years. It changed and strengthened each of us and bound us in a bond of love beyond anything we could have imagined. It brought us happiness and new friends. As I write these last lines, I am watching Frank teach Aileen's grandson Phillip to sail. A postcard from Alison, my mother's baby-sitting charge, lies on the desk in front of me. Up north, Gladys and John are packing their case for a holiday with us, and Frank and I have revived the dreams we abandoned over six years ago. The sun shines, the flowers bloom and the birds sing. We have every happiness. God bless Adeline.

Postscript from Frank

I have always looked on death as a renewal of life. I have always found it difficult to take part in the rigmarole of death which those who are left alive indulge themselves in—the weeping, the mourning, the funeral charade, the obituaries and the stone monuments are all for us, and not for the dead person. She is beyond it all, passing through the last, wonderful adventure whose joys and sufferings can never be told.

Adeline looked quite wonderful when Wendy had laid her out on her bed, surrounded by her own memorabilia—her furniture, her photographs, her pictures, her clock—and her own dressing-gown hanging behind the door. I saw her twice more before she was lowered into the grave but she never looked as beautiful again as at that moment. Her features had fallen into a soft repose—the strength and forcefulness in her face was clear to see but now these were smoothed by a strange touch of compassion and of tenderness—an expression I had seen flit across her face at odd times during her life. Wendy has the same features; the same expression sometimes comes to her.

As she went about the business of laying her mother out, something which, as a nurse, she has done a thousand times, she wept silently and softly to herself, the tears rolling down her cheeks in rivulets. The tears were for her grief, I believe, but also they were tears of relief. A great work she had undertaken had been brought to a proper conclusion in a proper manner.

Adeline's death was a punctuation in our lives, a full stop—after it we start again. The future is full of promise.

"And death once dead," Shakespeare wrote, "there's no more dying then."

177

Epilogue

Wendy writes

Our story is not unique. It is happening now in thousands of homes all over the country where families and single women or men care for elderly people handicapped by senility, Alzheimer's disease, mental handicap or communication difficulties such as those my mother suffered. Now more women care for elderly dependants than care for young children and it will increase because the number of elderly dependants is rising rapidly.

Our story is not entirely typical because we enjoyed privileges many carers do not have. I was able to keep my job because of its flexibility in how and where I worked and through the support of colleagues and both editors of *Nursing Times*. My job provided essential respite from continual caring as well as the money to afford holidays and occasional free weekends. We had savings to fund initial large expenses and to tide us over until we were awarded disablement benefits and finally managed to make less expensive arrangements. My mother tried to co-operate as best she could. She retained an attractiveness and charm that frequently saved the day.

I had skills acquired in childhood by helping my mother with my grandmother and later in training as a nurse. We had family and friends who helped when and how they could. Most important of all, I had the support of a husband willing to listen and comfort as well as to give practical help by washing, ironing, cooking meals and even helping my mother.

Our story demonstrates how little the statutory services have to offer the severely dependent. Despite this we were able to provide my mother with twenty-four-hour care at home without abandoning our own lives. Central and local government could and should find ways to extend this possibility to all carers.

No carer should be expected to take a dependant home from hospital without having been taught how to nurse, lift and handle their dependant or having had the opportunity to practise. This should be part of the standard discharge procedure for every hospital patient. Every ward should also carry a range of relevant educational material for patients and relatives. The Health Education Authority with the assistance of relevant voluntary organisations should consider how this can be done.

All carers and their dependants need respite from each other and no carer should be forced to give up a job. Employers should be encouraged to allow carers the equivalent of maternity leave in which to make suitable arrangements. They may also need help to move to part-time work or job-sharing arrangements. As firms change to the more flexible European system of a specified number of hours in a year rather than a day, some employees should have more freedom to tailor their working hours to their domestic arrangements.

The state services will never be able to supply all the help necessary; therefore health and social services, and possibly the Manpower Services Commission, should have responsibility to see that carers and elderly people are provided with advice and assistance to employ private help when they need it. It is not easy to advertise, interview or teach a helper. Uncertainty over the PAYE and National Insurance position, or the prospect of administering it, is a deterrent to many who could otherwise afford some help. There are untapped sources of expertise and help among the newly retired and ex-carers which could be used beneficially. Research into satisfactory private caring arrangements is likely to be revealing about how and where services could be focused.

Dependent old people should not be left in sole charge of an unsupported unsupervised housekeeper. Where there are no responsible relatives or where they are uninterested or seldom visit, some form of supervision and support should be provided. Old people are vulnerable and a paid housekeeper suffers the same stresses and strains as other carers. Local authorities register and supervise child minders. Old people deserve similar protection.

There must be thought too for the next generation of carers.

Fewer children have an opportunity to absorb the skills and attitudes necessary for home nursing and care, once a part of every housewife's experience. New ways can be found. Old people and young children enjoy each other's company and imaginative ways for them to help one another should be encouraged by parents, schools, residential homes and hospitals.

Relatives, friends and neighbours are the country's largest asset in supporting the growing number of dependants but too often they are left to 'get on with it'. Increasingly we hear of old people pushed out of hospital to relatives who do not want them or cannot cope. Many people would be shocked to discover the extent of deprivation locally among old people and their carers.

Local communities and their newspapers should demand much more revealing public reports from health and local authorities. Instead of studying meaningless balance sheets they should demand to know how standards of care are measured and how their local services compare nationally. One recognised measure of nursing care called Monitor has highlighted hospitals where patients receive less than half the necessary nursing care—this does not appear in the health authority's annual report.

Press reporters should ask how many patients are allocated to each nurse rather than how many nurses the authority employs. They should ask how many people have been refused home helps rather than how much more money has been put into the service. They should seek to discover how many people have been placed in residential care because relatives had no support.

Local clubs and voluntary organisations need encouragement to take some interest in their elderly members and their families. It is also possible that local enterprise boards and the Co-operative Development Agency could help develop services to fill some of the gaps as building societies and property developers are doing in providing sheltered accommodation for a similar market.

Points for Carers

VISITING A PATIENT IN HOSPITAL

The support of relatives and friends can be vital to the recovery, quality of future life or peaceful death of an ill patient. You can contribute firstly by asking whether there are guidelines for relatives—some hospitals provide them, particularly in children's wards and intensive care units. They will be more likely to be provided in all wards if relatives and patients request them.

Give the doctors and nurses as much information as possible about the patient's illness, interests, lifestyle and any peculiar habits. Tell the staff if you notice changes in how your relative behaves or talks—as they have not known the patient previously, they are less likely to notice. Check that the patient has and is using dentures, glasses, hearing aid and any other aids or equipment used at home.

Give comfort and security by sitting with the patient. If he is very ill or weak, take some sort of occupation such as knitting or the crossword. This removes the need to talk which is more relaxing for patient and visitor. Avoid smoking or wearing heavy scent—it can be nauseating. Do not pass remarks about a sleeping or unconscious patient as he may be able to hear and understand.

If the patient has difficulty feeding and it is possible to visit at mealtimes, ask whether you can help. Even if the nurses attend to this, you will have more time to devote to it. Favourite foods cooked at home may tempt a poor appetite—check first that they are allowed.

If the patient is having help from the physiotherapist, speech therapist or occupational therapist, ask them how you can help your relative's progress—you may be able to carry out exercises or other activities at visiting time.

Ask the ward sister or the patient's regular nurse whether there is anything you can contribute to make your relative more comfortable—good-quality disposable incontinence pads might be preferable to grapes.

An old person will be less likely to become disorientated if relatives can bring in family photographs, pets or children to visit, the daily and local paper, and a hand mirror to see themselves. Talk about familiar people, events or things at home. Correct any confused remarks, encourage listening to and watching favourite soap operas or regular radio and television favourites. Take your relative into the hospital grounds, out for a drive to a familiar place or out to tea.

Ask the pastor or representative of the patient's religion how you can help if the patient is a believer and wants spiritual solace. Reading *The Bible* or favourite holy book may give the patient comfort. You do not have to share the belief.

All this is not a pipe-dream. It is possible for relatives to be fully involved in hospital care as Valerie Gilbert, sister in charge of a ward for the elderly at the Queen's Medical Centre, Nottingham, shows in this extract from her letter published in *Nursing Times*, 2 April 1986:

"We allow unrestricted visiting at any time, day or night. We openly encourage it for the following reasons.

1. The relatives of our patients do not have the worry of remembering visiting times.

2. The elderly visitors can use their free bus passes at the relevant times.

3. Our city consists of many people working shifts so open visiting is convenient to their needs.

4. The elderly visitors need not worry about travelling in the dark, winter evenings.

5. Our patients have a need to see as many members of their family and friends as possible in the latter years of their lives.

6. We see the ward as belonging to the patients not to the staff.

We have had relatives bringing in patients' favourite food

183

at breakfast time, and sandwiches and flasks of drink, so that they can stay longer with the patient.

The patients are encouraged to wear their own clothes, to maintain their identity and dignity. The relatives escort the patient to X-ray and other departments in the hospital. The consultant sees the relatives as well as the patients in his ward round.

Recently we had a wife who stayed by her husband's side for four months. She brought in a fold-up bed and slept at his side nightly. She assisted in the washing and feeding of him until the day he died. She and I then performed the last offices together.

We see the relatives as contributing to the nursing care of the patients and as members of our team. We find their participation is an effective way of reducing their anxiety and is an aid to communication with the staff."

MAKING A COMPLAINT

If you are unhappy about the care your relative is receiving in hospital, the procedure to follow may be outlined in the hospital information booklet usually found in the patient's locker. If there is none, it is best to begin by speaking to the ward sister or charge nurse, explaining your worries as nicely as possible. In a well-managed hospital your complaint will be welcomed, investigated and put right. If at all possible, try to get it put right at this level and to maintain goodwill.

If you are not satisfied, ask for the name of the general manager and write to him. If you feel unable to do this, discuss your difficulties with the secretary of the Community Health Council—the address can be found in the local library, the telephone directory or from the Citizen's Advice Bureau. The Community Health Council is there to represent the public. They will not complain for you but they will advise and help you.

If you are not satisfied with the general manager's response, write to the Health Service Ombudsman. He will only investigate after you have raised the matter with the general manager of the health authority concerned. He cannot yet investigate criticism of a doctor's diagnosis and treatment.

England: Office of Health Service Ombudsman
Church House
Great Smith Street
London SW1P 3BW
Telephone: 01–212 1785

Wales: 3rd Floor
Queen's Court
Plymouth Street
Cardiff CF1 4AD
Telephone: 0222–3946 21

Scotland: 11 Melville Crescent
Edinburgh EH3 7L4
Telephone: 031–225 7456

Other organisations which help are as follows.

The Patients' Association
Room 33
18 Charing Cross Road
London WC2H 0HR
Telephone: 01–240 0671
(exists to fight for patients' rights)

Action for the Victims of Medical Accidents (AVMA)
24 Southwark Street
London SE1 1TY
Telephone: 01–403 4744

If you have no complaints but would like to suggest improvements, put your suggestions in the suggestion box if there is one, or send them to the Community Health Council. If you are pleased with the care, tell the staff and try to find time to write to the general manager. It helps staff morale to know their efforts are appreciated.

FINDING A RESIDENTIAL HOME

There are two kinds of residential home.

(1) *Nursing homes* are for people who need nursing care. There is a qualified nurse on duty at all times. Most are privately owned

by commercial organisations or charities, a few are run by the NHS, and all are registered by the local health authority.

(2) *Residential or rest homes* are for elderly people no longer able to cope with running a home but not needing more nursing care than the district nurse can provide in their own homes. They are owned and managed by either commercial organisations or the local authority. All are registered by the local authority social services department. To avoid elderly people having to move from one type of home to another, some homes are jointly registered as both nursing and residential homes.

Make a start by asking the local authority social services department for a list of homes—the list will include nursing and rest homes. The more helpful authorities provide basic information about the homes, such as approximate cost, whether the rooms are single or shared, and whether personal items of furniture are allowed.

Decide how much you or your relative can pay (DHSS help is available for those on a low income). Consider what kind of facilities you would like—near to shops and recreation facilities, near to public transport, and able to bring your own furniture. Match this against what you know of the homes and short-list several for visiting. Always remember you are choosing a home and it is the preference of the person who will live there that counts. If at all possible, take your relative to see the homes and choose which he or she likes.

When visiting, ask questions—make a list beforehand of queries such as arrangements for medical care and incontinence, programme of activities, outings and visits, who visits (chiropodist, dentist, hairdresser, occupational therapist or speech therapist), whether personal furniture and television are allowed and whether pets are allowed. Ask to see the menu for the past week. Can relatives stay and help with an ill or dying patient?

Observe and talk to other residents. Are they happy, content and occupied or sitting, sleepy, apathetic and silent? Is the place homely? Are there plants and flowers, a dog or cat? Can residents participate in the running of the home by joining in domestic chores or weeding the garden? Is there a residents' committee?

Most homes allow or encourage a trial period of a couple of weeks. This enables the person to see whether he or she likes it and it enables other residents to offer objections. Do not relinquish a lease or sell a home until you are quite certain the new arrangement is working.

FINDING HELP

There are three main sources of help: firstly, relatives, friends and neighbours, secondly, state services and voluntary organisations and, lastly, private help. You should make the most of all three—trying to cope alone is to invite disaster.

Relatives, friends and neighbours

Reactions to illness and handicap vary; so do not be surprised if a close relative rejects the dependant and a neighbour on nodding terms turns out to be an ally. The more handicapped or confused the dependant, the more continued visiting and support will depend on you acting as a link. Most people feel happier with a practical task—Jane is much more likely to visit dotty old Gran every week if she goes to wash and set her hair. If anyone offers to help, try to suggest a practical task within their capabilities. It avoids the strain of having to maintain a relationship entirely through conversation, is stimulating for the old person and is satisfying for the helper. It helps to make a list of jobs with the names of possible helpers beside them.

Jobs that relatives, friends, neighbours or a volunteer can do

Wash and set hair; manicure nails.
Make appointment to take to the hairdresser, shopping, to a place of worship, to visit another friend, for a walk or to the library.
Play games such as cards, draughts, chess. Guessing games such as I Spy help recall and speech.
Read aloud or bring some music of the old person's preference.
Help to write a letter to a distant friend or relative.
Take for a drive or out to tea.
Bring an animal or a baby to visit.
Help to choose and wrap presents or to write cards for relatives, friends, or helpers at anniversaries or birthdays.
Make the tea or prepare a light meal and share it with the old person.

187

State services and services from voluntary organisations

The following should be available locally.

Home helps

Home helps are provided by the local authority social services department. They will do essential household chores as directed by their organiser—these may not always be what you would like help with. Charges vary throughout the country; in some areas the service is free. In most places there are not sufficient numbers to meet demands and the organiser decides which clients have priority and how many hours can be provided.

Home nurses

Home nurses are provided free of charge by the local health authority. They are usually based in the health centre, the family doctor's surgery or the child health clinic. They will do dressings and give injections and enemas and so on in the home. They will help with bathing and washing which is usually delegated to an auxiliary helper. Some places have an evening service to help old people to bed and a night service for very ill patients.

Care assistants

Care assistants may be known by various other titles. In a few areas the home help and nursing auxiliary job has been combined and extended so that the helper can give personal assistance with washing and bathing as well as try to involve the elderly person in household activities, to encourage independence and mobility. Information about such services should be available from the social services or district nursing service. This service may also be provided at unsocial hours—evenings and weekends.

Loan of equipment

Commodes, backrests, cradles, bathing aids and so on are available on loan, usually from the social services department, community nurses or through a voluntary organisation such as the Red Cross. There may be a small charge. If building work or alterations to the home are needed, these can be arranged through the social services department. Borrowed equipment should be returned when it is no longer needed.

Sitting service

A sitting service is to relieve carers while they shop or have an evening out. These are usually provided by a voluntary organisation the best known being Crossroads. The Salvation Army, the Red Cross, the WRVS, local churches, Age Concern and others may provide such facilities. Information should be available from the local social services department.

Respite care

Respite care is to enable carers to have a break or a holiday. The family doctor or social worker can arrange admission for the dependant to a local hospital, social services old peoples' home, a private nursing home or to a local family. Some voluntary organisations may be able to arrange for a helper to live in the home while the carer is away. Staying with a relative or live-in help is the least disturbing for elderly confused dependants and is likely to cause least problems for the carer on her return.

Information about the range of state and voluntary services locally and how to contact them should be available from the social services department, the library or the Citizen's Advice Bureau or listed in the telephone directory *Yellow Pages*.

Private help

First decide what help you need which cannot be provided by the state services—occasional or full-time domestic help, nursing care or both. A domestic employment agency or nursing agency may be able to supply what you need. Their charges and service vary. Some may require the patient to take direct responsibility for paying a helper, including PAYE and National Insurance. The telephone directory *Yellow Pages* will list local agencies. The jobcentre can send people for interview free of charge but they do not administer National Insurance or tax. They can give you

189

advice on the current legal responsibilities of employers—part-time workers and pensioners carry few responsibilities.

Finding your own help will cost less and be most likely to meet your requirements. Similar jobs advertised in the local paper will indicate the current rates of payment. Compose an advertisement to attract only the people you want. If possible, include a telephone number. You may get a response through placing it in local shops but the local paper is likely to attract more replies. Arrange to be near your telephone on the day of publication and the following few days. Make a list of relevant questions which will weed out unsuitable applicants. For example, if there is heavy lifting, you do not want someone with back strain.

Find out a few details from callers before explaining the job; otherwise you may spend five minutes outlining the job only to find the person lives miles away or is on night duty and thinks your job can be fitted in afterwards. If the caller sounds suitable and finds the rate of pay acceptable, arrange for her to come and see you. You may want to ask for references. These can help but they can also be misleading. Always interview a prospective helper in the presence of the person who needs help. Do not employ anyone an old person has not met and found acceptable. Even if communication with or the mental faculties of the old person are impaired, it gives a chance to see whether the old person likes the helper and for you to observe the helper's reaction to the old person. It demonstrates to prospective helpers that the old person holds a respected position in the family and you expect her to be treated accordingly. It gives an opportunity to observe the old person's reaction to the prospective helper and vice versa.

Look for someone who talks to the old person normally, telling her about themselves and their family, someone who can understand the importance of involving her in the daily chores which she may enjoy but cannot do alone—washing-up, dusting and so on. Look for helpers who, when the chores are done, will sit and talk, read aloud or play a game. It may be useful to organise interviews so that you can chat to the applicant with the old person present and then leave them together while you make a cup of tea.

During your chat, explore all the possibilities. Will she be able to come at the times needed? Would she be free occasionally at other times if you wanted to have an evening out or a weekend off? Has she small children who may become ill or need attention? Children do not have to be a problem—helpers sometimes bring them and, as old people often enjoy children, occasionally it can work well. Make sure the applicant understands the conditions you are offering—the hours required and whether payment is for hours worked only, which is normal for part-time jobs.

Most applicants are female but an elderly man might prefer the company of a male assistant, particularly where the burden of care falls on a daughter or daughter-in-law which can be embarrassing. Even if an applicant seems suitable and wants the job, never accept anyone on the spot. You need time to discover the old person's reaction and there may be other applicants to see. Explain this and say when you will be able to let the applicant know. Afterwards it is useful to write down your impressions and some relevant facts in a book; otherwise you may become muddled if there are several people to see.

Once you select your preferred applicant, offer her (or him) the job on condition that the arrangement terminates if it is not satisfactory for either party. Interviews are false situations and it takes a week or two to see whether the arrangement works. It is unpleasant to be dependent for intimate help on someone who is unsympathetic to you. People who seem acceptable to you may not be acceptable to the old person.

No one will do everything exactly the way you do but only you can decide what is acceptable. You will probably want to draw the line somewhere between perfection and broken dishes at every meal, shrunken woollies, and everything put away in the wrong places. To avoid some of this, it is helpful to add strong likes and dislikes, such as not to use Vim on the bath, to a written account of what the job includes. This is helpful as it avoids mis-understandings between you and the helper about what is expected.

Keep the names, addresses and telephone numbers of all interested applicants whether you have seen them or not. Explain that someone is trying the job but that, if it does not work out, you may contact them again. This saves advertising. It is helpful to keep a book with details of all suitable applicants as some may still be available even months later.

If the old person cannot explain how she likes things done,

demonstrate the routine on the first morning. She may be able to communicate by other means but it will take a stranger some time to recognise the signals. Try to be in the house at least for the first day. Do not assume that someone with qualifications or experience in relevant work can manage without a demonstration and do not allow yourself or your dependant to be dominated by a helper who thinks she knows best—you are the employer. It can be useful to have a written account (see page 107) of the routine to refer to—it is difficult to remember everything. It is also a useful reminder if a helper has been away or comes infrequently.

Full-time twenty-four-hour help is the most difficult to arrange and needs serious consideration. Remember it will be just as tedious and tiring for a paid help to look after an elderly person as it is for a relative. The more difficult the dependant, the less likely the arrangement will last. Even if you find someone acceptable, your employee will want time off each week and paid holidays. You will have to make additional arrangements for this.

You will be responsible for tax, National Insurance, sickness benefit and so on. This will add at least 25% extra to the basic salary you offer while tax allowance for a housekeeper is negligible. Household expenses in food, electricity and gas are likely to rise considerably.

The local jobcentre will be able to supply a range of up-to-date Department of Employment leaflets on the responsibilities of employers and employees' rights. Another useful source is the National Federation for Self Employed and Small Businesses (140 Lower Marsh, London SE1 7AE). Advice on National Insurance and tax is available from the local DHSS and tax offices, but these are complicated to administer and you may have to employ an accountant or wages clerk. A contract of employment is also advisable and you may need a solicitor to draw this up.

Another way to provide twenty-four-hour care is to offer free accommodation in return for some help in the evening or at night while paid part-time help covers the day. Alternatively the whole twenty-four hours can be covered by three or four part-timers as described on page 131. An old person often enjoys a change of face. If disabilities are restrictive, a change of person means more variety and nobody becomes bored or irritated.

It is useful to keep a diary with rotas, hours and messages about the day's activities. The front page should include the telephone numbers of everyone, where they can be contacted in an emergency and the doctor's telephone number. This is essential in case anyone is late or, if there is a problem, the helper in the house will know who to contact.

Do not be discouraged by failures. You will be very lucky to find the perfect helper first time. In the end, someone suitable will always turn up but prepare yourself for disappointments—those who fail to arrive on the first morning with no telephone call or explanation, or those who start off well but soon get tired and cannot be bothered. This is to be expected. When it happens, try not to dwell on it but start to look for someone else.

If you are considerate towards your helpers, you are well on the way to having a happy stable home, but do not expect them to get on with things indefinitely. No system will work without regular supervision.

ESTABLISHING A ROUTINE AT HOME

The routine you adopt can create drudgery or happiness. The physical or mental incapacities of your dependant have created the circumstances you both live in—it is easy to let them dominate your lives to the exclusion of all else. Both you and your dependant need social and intellectual stimulation independent of each other. You both need a sense of purpose and belonging and you must create a lifestyle which allows for these needs.

If the carer makes all the sacrifices, the dependant will soon feel a burden and lose any sense of usefulness. This leads to apathy and depression which hastens senility and the dependant becomes increasingly forgetful, unreliable, awkward and aggressive. This makes life difficult for the carer who may lose control and injure the dependant no matter how loving the relationship. Resentment mounts and the carer loses respect and love for the dependant. This is a tragedy which will destroy the relationship and leave the carer guilty when the dependant dies. By contrast the dependant who retains some responsibilities, however small, will feel happier, the carer's life is easier and their relationship better.

You must create a routine for your lives which includes breaks from each other—for the carer a paid or voluntary job, visits to friends or relatives, personal shopping trips and holidays away from the dependant. This is why you must make full use of every possible assistance whether from family, from the state, from voluntary agencies or paid privately. You must apply for all available benefits to help to pay for the relief and you must organise it before you get too tired and it becomes beyond your capabilities.

If you have a job, try to enlist the support of your employer. You may want to take time off, unpaid if necessary, to make suitable arrangements or you might be able to rearrange your hours or change to another job in the same organisation. Do not assume that there is no alternative but to give up.

If you do not have a job, try to get involved in something away from your dependant. You might help with one of the voluntary services or there may be a carer's group in your vicinity. To talk to other carers, to hear their views and feelings or to pick up ideas from them is comforting and removes the feeling of isolation common among carers. The National Council for Carers and their Elderly Dependants has branches all over the country. There may be one nearby which you can join or you could help to organise one locally. You may even want to swap responsibilities with another carer for an afternoon or so weekly. One of my best helpers was herself a carer. She found it a great relief to get away for three mornings weekly while someone else looked after her father.

Your dependant's week will be most successful if it follows a regular routine. This gives a sense of security and removes the need for a failing memory to have to think what to do next. A regular weekly and daily routine helps an old person to retain a grip on life. Domestic routine provides markers—Monday washing, Tuesday ironing, Wednesday the lunch club and so on. Similarly the hours of the day should have a pattern—up at 8.30 am, coffee at 11 am, lunch at 1 pm, tea at 4 pm, supper at 7 pm and bed at 10 pm.

While this gives a structure, each part of the routine should have a purpose to be achieved at the dependant's own pace so that life remains purposeful and physically tiring. The old person sleeps and eats better and feels happier, and physical and mental failings are contained. Generally the day should include some domestic chores, some leisure and some social exchange.

Any routine should aim to keep a dependant as active and involved as possible. Seek advice from a physiotherapist and occupational therapist—your family doctor can put you in touch with them. It can be difficult to persuade helpers that it is better to leave the chores until the old person is ready to help. It is also time consuming to get an old person involved and to work out how to bridge some of the gaps. Simple changes can make all the difference—moving the dishes to a ground-level cupboard so that a wheelchair-bound person can reach them, moving the furniture slightly to give strategic support if walking is unsteady, moving the table nearer the sink or sticking hooks within reach.

An occupational therapist can assess how the home can be made more convenient but it is difficult to see everything. It is the person most familiar with the daily routine who sees small changes which make life easier. There may be many jobs the old person cannot manage alone but can assist with.

Initially the preparation to enable an old person to carry out a task is more time consuming than doing it oneself. For example, for a one-handed person to wash smalls, if the sink is inaccessible, you may have to prepare the water, to roll up the dependant's sleeves, to arrange the basin within reach, to provide a tray to prevent clothes from dripping on the floor, to change each rinsing water, to help to turn garments inside out, to help to roll down sleeves and to dry hands. This takes twice as long as doing the job oneself.

Try to set small goals for each task. In this example, aim first for your dependant to find the bowl—you may have to move it to a more accessible place. When this has been achieved, can she fill it with water? She may not be able to move a full bowl of water but she could manage to fill it in position with a jug. In this way she can gradually master each part of the task until she is able to wash smalls alone. This is a triumph for the dependant who has now become a real help with the chores and it shows a worthwhile investment of your time. A dependant's preferences and capabilities will influence what they want to be involved in but always be alert for small initiatives and encourage them. Gradually you may be able to build up a number of chores which your dependant likes and can manage alone or with help.

Leisure activities do not have to stop at television—aimlessly watching programme after programme is stupefying. Try to find other alternatives—books, card games, gardening even if only growing seeds on a window sill or weeding a window-box, feeding wild birds or grooming a pet. Books and recordings of music or stories can be borrowed from the library and a local toy library may be able to lend some suitable puzzles or games. There may also be a jigsaw puzzle library you can join.

Try to arrange some social exchange with others outside the home as often as you can each week. This is where relatives, neighbours and volunteers can help—granddaughter Jane for hair washing, Mrs Pike from the church for reading aloud or a car drive, and the next-door neighbour to come and make a cup of tea.

It may seem an almost impossible task to arrange such a variety of activities for a dependant. You may have to push and encourage your dependant and to jolly your helpers along. However, once it becomes established, it is surprising how it continues by its own momentum. It will provide the respite you both need from each other. Without this, boredom sets in, the sense of purpose disappears, and dependant and carer deteriorate.

DRUGS

Drugs can be the downfall of any system, their adverse effects making life impossible for carer and dependant. Try to avoid giving drugs to old people. They take too many drugs; indeed 10% of hospital admissions among the elderly are caused by drugs. At present the average person over seventy-five years takes one drug regularly and a third take four or five drugs daily. These may conflict with each other, particularly where care is fragmented and different drugs are prescribed by different doctors for different diseases. This is further complicated by taking non-prescribed over-the-counter drugs for indigestion, heartburn, constipation or aches and pains—often reactions to prescribed drugs.

Drugs may not be absorbed, particularly if laxatives are overused. The likelihood of reactions increase rapidly with age and may be worse than the disease they are supposed to relieve. If they make the dependant confused, drowsy, difficult or unsteady as sedatives, tranquillisers or anti-depressants in particular do, they increase the carer's work and responsibility. She may not be able to cope and the dependant has to be admitted to residential care.

196

Drugs should only be used if they improve the quality of life. If they are taken, ensure they are properly used and stored. Encourage a dependant to manage his own drugs as long as possible but see that it is made easy. Choose a long-acting daily dose in preference to three or four doses daily. Medicines should be reasonably pleasant to take and liquid rather than tablets if there is difficulty in swallowing. Discuss such possibilities with your dependant's doctor.

When a doctor prescribes a drug, make sure you know what it is for, what he expects it to do and the possible side-effects— drowsiness, headaches, dizziness or nausea. How often is it to be taken and are these times vital? Should the drug be taken before or after food and will it be affected by any non-prescribed drugs such as aspirin or any foods, alcohol or sunlight.

Some doctors and chemists issue instruction leaflets—ask if you are not given one. The bottle or packet label should be typed with clear instructions, the name of the drug, when to take it and when it expires. A screw or cap container is easiest to manage, provided that there are no children in the house. If requested, store in the refrigerator, a cool place or out of the sunlight; otherwise they will be ineffective. Do not accept repeat prescriptions—ask the doctor to re-assess whether the drugs are still needed and for how long. Many drugs continue to be prescribed long after they are effective and continual repeated doses can cause serious illness.

When an old person's drugs are changed, discontinued or restarted, be alert for any changes in behaviour, rashes, headaches and so on and report them to the doctor. If drugs are discontinued or past their expiry date, return them to the chemist for disposal.

DYING

Given the choice, most people would choose to die at home in familiar, safe surroundings. In practice, 60–70% die in hospitals although this may be changing as the idea of a pain-free peaceful death spreads in the setting-up of hospice care to help people to die at home or in a homely residential setting where relatives can easily be involved.

Dying at home enables loved ones to be much more involved in practical care. This helps later when the bereaved are able to remember the help and comfort they gave. Loved ones who are excluded from care usually have more difficulty in accepting the death and recovering from their grief.

All of us are going to die and it is best to prepare in good time. Death is part of life to be planned for just as birth, education and marriage. To dismiss it as morbid and distasteful can lead to hurried, ill-informed decisions which are regretted later.

Try to talk about the arrangements with your dependant. Where would she (or he) like to die? Does she (or he) want to be cremated or buried? How should the body or ashes be disposed of? Ask the family doctor or the district nurse what help they can give. Do the district nurses provide a night service or can they arrange funding for a private agency nurse if necessary?

Find out about local undertakers, how much they charge and what they provide. Find out about council rulings in the cemetery. Many operate rigid systems forbidding flowers to be planted or monuments other than a standard pattern. Bereaved relatives may find this out when it is too late and be left feeling helpless and bitter.

The care of a dying person will vary somewhat according to their illness but, if you have been looking after your dependant, you should be able to cope at home with the advice and help of the family doctor and the district nurse or the hospice team if there is one locally. Do not assume that your relatives will be more comfortable in hospital. Even the most caring doctors and nurses cannot provide the love and peace of home and familiar family and friends.

Ask the nurses to show you what to do. Remember the main aim is to keep your dependant comfortable and not to prolong life. Skin, breathing, bladder, bowels and mouth are the main points to observe. To keep the skin free of pressure sores, your dependant's position should be moved two-hourly to a different position in the bed or onto a chair or sofa. Wash and dry carefully any sweaty parts such as under the arms or folds of the skin and, if too hot or too cold, increase or decrease the blankets accordingly. An upright position helps breathing and prevents chest infections. See that the bladder is emptied every four hours and the bowels move at least every three days. If you think the results look or smell strange, save some in a clean yogurt or margarine carton to show the doctor or nurse. Fluids such as milk, fruit juice or water help to keep the bladder, bowels and mouth comfortable. If a couple of teaspoons of glucose are added, it is easily absorbed by the old person and gives a little energy. Mouthwashes and glycerine or Vaseline on the lips help to keep them moist and free of sores. The doctor can control any pain with drugs.

Sit with your dependant as much as possible. A rota of relatives and other helpers will relieve the strain. Touch is reassuring and becomes increasingly important as your dependant grows weaker and finds it exhausting to talk.

Keep the doctor involved and inform him or her when your dependant dies. The doctor will visit and certify the death, issuing you with a death certificate to be taken to the Registrar of Births, Deaths and Marriages. The body will start to cool and stiffen within an hour to twenty-four hours. If the district nurse is not immediately available, you should close the eyelids, lay the body flat, straighten the limbs and insert any dentures if desired. Prop the chin with a pillow to keep the mouth closed. Insert an incontinence pad or a piece of plastic and some absorbent material under the body to protect the bed in case urine seeps away.

The body must be prepared for burial or cremation by an undertaker or someone who knows how to lay the body out, but it is possible for relatives to help or to do it themselves. In Britain, this is generally left to the undertaker and it can be quite difficult to arrange anything other than what the local undertaker provides. This is why it is advisable to investigate local provision beforehand so that you can make other plans if you wish.

The Registrar of Births, Deaths and Marriages will issue a certificate of disposal to enable burial to proceed or cremation to be applied for. He will also issue a Certificate of Registration of Death which enables the estate to be settled. His office usually provides helpful leaflets, explaining how to proceed.

It can take a year or more for the pain of bereavement to ease. It is a subject well researched and written about and it can help to read some of the many available books. Never be ashamed to express your grief by weeping, by talking, by pilgrimages to the cemetery or in whatever way you want. If it stays bottled up inside, your grief may be slow to leave.

If you believe state and private services are inadequate, you can help to bring about changes by lobbying your member of parliament and local councillors, by joining a carer's group and putting your ideas forward with others, and by alerting your trade union to the needs of carers who have jobs.

List of Useful Addresses

There are many agencies offering help and advice of one kind or another. The small selection below should point you to others appropriate to your circumstances.

Age Concern
Bernard Sunley House
60 Pitcairn Road
Mitcham
Surrey
Telephone: 01–640 5431

National centre for advice and information on all aspects of care for the elderly, which produces a range of leaflets and booklets including a yearly publication *Your Rights* for pensioners.

Chest, Heart and Stroke
  Association
Tavistock House North
Tavistock Square
London WC1 9JE
Telephone: 01–387 3012

Offers advice, books, leaflets and regular journals for stroke patients and their carers. Information about stroke clubs and volunteer schemes to help stroke patients with speech and other problems in their homes or through clubs.

Counsel and Care for the
  Elderly
131 Middlesex Street
London E1 7JF
Telephone: 01–621 1624 (case
  work department)

Provides individual advice for an elderly person or carer. In contact with other agencies for the elderly. Can advise on and arrange financial help for care at home, in residential accommodation or for respite care. Offers expert advice on residential homes in Greater London.

Disabled Living Foundation
380–384 Harrow Road
London W9 2HU
Telephone: 01–289 6111

Provides an information service and exhibition of aids for the disabled. There is also a clothing and continence advisory service.

Holiday Care Service
2 Old Bank Chambers
Station Road
Horley
Surrey RH6 9HW
Telephone: 0293–774535

Funded by the English Tourist Board, British Rail and tour operators to give information about hotels, holiday centres and resorts with facilities for the disabled, mentally ill, mentally handicapped and low-income families. Can help to arrange financial assistance for such holidays.

MIND (National Association for Mental Health)
22 Harley Street
London W1N 2ED
Telephone: 01–637 0741

Concerned with the needs of the mentally ill and handicapped. Provides a variety of information and some residential care.

National Council for Carers and their Elderly Dependants
29 Chilworth Mews
London W2 3RG
Telephone: 01–724 7776

Offers help, advice and support for carers. Has local branches throughout the country. A regular newsletter is full of useful contributions from carers themselves.

The Court of Protection
25 Store Street
London WC1E 7BP
Telephone: 01–636 6877

Information on power of attorney and the legal position when someone can no longer manage their financial affairs.

List of Books

The medicine and social service shelves in the public library are good sources of relevant books. The reference library will have up-to-date directories of organisations who can help. If necessary, ask the librarian to help you find them.

GENERAL REFERENCES

Law, D., and Paterson, B. (1980). *Living after a Stroke*, Human Horizon Series, Souvenir Press.
Murphy, D. (1979). *Wheels within Wheels*, John Murray.

OTHER BOOKS

Beck, M., and Barker, H. (1985). *Nutrition and Dietetics for Nurses*, Churchill Livingstone.
Gray, M., and McKenzie, H. (1980). *Take Care of Your Elderly Relative*, George Allen and Unwin.
Irvine, R. E., Bagnall, M. K., Smith, B. J., and Bishop, V. A. (1986). *The Older Patient—An Introduction to Geriatric Nursing*, 4th edn, Hodder and Stoughton.
Isted, C. (1979). *Learning to Speak Again After a Stroke*, King Edwards Hospital Fund.
Kubler-Ross, E. (1986). *Death—The Final Stage of Growth*, A Touchstone Book, Simon and Schuster, New York.
Lamerton, R. (1980). *Care of the Dying*, Pelican.
Mace, Robins, Castleton, Cloke and McEwan (1985). *The 36 Hour Day, Caring at Home for Confused Elderly People*, Hodder and Stoughton with Age Concern.

Practical Nursing—The Basic Guide to Nursing the Family (1984), British Red Cross.

Wilson, M. (1984). *The College of Health Guide to Homes for Elderly People*, College of Health, 18 Victoria Park Square, Bethnal Green, London E2 9PF.

Index